Culinary Arts Institute

MICROWAVE COOKING

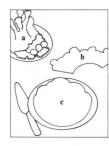

Featured in cover photo:
a. Pork Roast, 37
b. Cooked Fresh Broccoli, 58
c. Pineapple Upside-Down Cake, 82

MICROWAVE COOKING

MICROWAVE COOKING

The Culinary Arts Institute Staff:

Helen Geist: Director • Sherrill Corley: Editor
Helen Lehman: Assistant Editor • Barbara Harris: Consultant
Edward Finnegan: Executive Editor • Charles Bozett: Art Director
Ethel La Roche: Editorial Assistant • Ivanka Simatic: Recipe Tester
Malinda Miller: Copy Editor • John Mahalek: Art Assembly

Book designed and coordinated by Charles Bozett and Laurel DiGangi

Illustrations by Joanna Adamska-Koperska

Photographs by Zdenek Pivecka

Adventures in Cooking SERIES

Culinary Arts Institute
1727 South Indiana Avenue, Chicago, Illinois 60616

CONTENTS

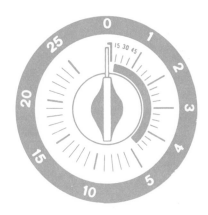

INTRODUCTION TO MICROWAVE COOKING

Microwave ovens are making cooking fun, fast, and efficient. Once you learn the basics of microwave ovens, you'll wonder how you ever cooked without one.

As with any new appliance, it takes time and experience to learn to use a microwave oven to its fullest. But by starting with simple recipes, you will soon master the techniques of microwave magic. You will find that the microwave oven will cook about 75% of the foods usually cooked conventionally, making it a welcome addition to your kitchen. A few exceptions not suitable for microwave cooking are hard- and soft-cooked eggs in the shell, popovers, angel food cakes, and some yeast breads. Popping popcorn and home canning are not recommended. Microwaves are also very good for defrosting and reheating frozen foods, and for refreshing stale crackers, potato chips, cakes, and breads.

We recommend using your microwave for one or two items at mealtime, snack time, or baking time until you learn how microwaves affect food and what results to expect. Soon you will be adapting your own favorite recipes for preparation in the microwave oven.

HOW DO MICROWAVES WORK?
Microwaves are a form of radiant energy with a very high frequency and extremely short wavelength similar to infrared heat, visible light, and high-frequency radio waves. The magnetron tube in the microwave oven converts electricity to microwave energy. Microwaves have been assigned two frequencies, 915 MHZ and 2450 MHZ. The recipes in this book were tested using 600- to 650-watt ovens, with a frequency of 2450 MHZ.

Microwaves are able to pass directly through glass, paper, plastic, and some wood. They are reflected by metal surfaces. The walls of the oven cavity are metal to allow the microwaves to bounce off and come in contact with the food, where they are absorbed. When the microwaves hit water molecules in food, the molecules vibrate, causing friction between molecules, which creates heat within the food.

ADVANTAGES OF MICROWAVE COOKING
Speed. Most foods cook faster by microwave than by conventional methods, although some foods that are high in moisture or are very dense may be less quick-cooking. The amount of food in the oven also affects cooking time. When a large amount of food is being cooked, it is possible that the cooking time is not shorter than when conventional methods are used.

Convenience. Frozen foods are easily defrosted in the microwave when needed. No need to plan ahead, as with conventional cooking methods. When reheating foods for latecomers, microwave cooking helps foods retain the flavor and moisture that are often lost with the conventional reheating.

Coolness. With microwave cooking, the food gets hot but the kitchen, oven, baking dishes, utensils, and you stay cool. Some cooking containers will get hot because of the transfer of heat of the food to the dish, but the microwaves themselves do not heat the dish.

Cleanliness. The interior of the microwave oven remains cool, so spills do not bake on and may be wiped up with a damp cloth or paper towel. If any foods should stick on the oven walls, heating 1 cup of water for 2½ to 3 minutes produces steam which will soften the spills. The same dish can be used for both cooking and serving, so there are fewer dishes to wash. Cleaning baking dishes and mixing containers is easier and quicker too, because food does not stick to them, as it does in conventional cooking. It is advisable to keep the oven clean, because any food left on the walls or bottom of the oven will absorb microwaves, and increase cooking times.

Economy. Foods reheated in a microwave oven retain their fresh-cooked flavor, so are more likely to be saved for easy reheating. Leftovers may be frozen and easily heated for another meal. Microwave cooking is generally more electrically efficient than conventional ovens because microwave cooking usually requires only about half the energy used in conventional cooking. This is because microwaves are converted to heat directly within the food, so no heat is lost. However, when cooking large amounts of food, more energy may actually be used in the microwave oven than in a conventional oven or on top of the range. The microwave oven also saves energy because no preheating is necessary, and there is no cooling-off period as with the conventional oven, when heat is simply being wasted.

COOKING UTENSILS AND CONTAINERS

Generally glass, glass ceramic, paper, or plastics may be used. Any containers that are used must allow the microwaves to pass through the food. Metal containers will reflect the microwaves and therefore should not be used.

The muffin maker, cupcaker, and roasting rack are utensils designed especially for microwave oven use. They are nonmetal and cannot be used in conventional ovens.

The shape of the container should also be considered. Shallow containers produce better results than deep ones. Round shapes are better than square or rectangular dishes. Containers with corners have a tendency to overcook foods in the corners, because more microwave energy is absorbed there.

The following cookware should not be used in microwave ovens:

—Centura® dinnerware by Corning.
—Glass containers containing metallic oxide substances.
—Plastics, when cooking foods high in fat, because the dish will melt. Plastics, except melamine, are recommended only when heating for short times.
—Paper, when cooking foods high in fat or for a long time. If heated for a length of time, paper may ignite.
—Metal utensils or dishes with metal trim.

To determine whether a dish is suitable for use in the microwave oven, place 1 cup of tap water and the empty dish to be tested in the microwave oven. Heat for 30 seconds to 1 minute. If the water becomes hot and the dish does not, the dish is acceptable for microwave use. If the dish becomes hot, it cannot be used for microwave cooking. When testing dinnerware, test several pieces from the set. In some instances the plates may be used but the cups cannot. (Closed-handle cups from Corelle® Livingware by Corning cannot be used even though all other Corelle® is acceptable.)

FACTORS AFFECTING COOKING

In microwave cooking, time is the variable which affects the cooking, not temperature. All foods are not alike, and therefore do not heat alike. The time needed for cooking is related to characteristics of the food.

Composition of food. Sugars and fats absorb energy very quickly, so foods high in sugar or fat will cook more rapidly than foods high in liquid. Salt tends to interfere with microwaves when sprinkled on the outside of food. When seasoning with salt, either add at the end of cooking or stir into the food. Foods high in moisture (vegetables, meats, and beverages) require more cooking time than those with little moisture (breads, cakes, and cereal products).

Starting temperature. Warm food requires less time to cook than cold food.

Volume of food. As the amount of food being cooked increases, cooking time increases.

Density of food. The more dense an item is the longer it takes to be cooked. Meat is more dense than a cake and so requires more time to heat.

Shape of food. Evenly shaped foods cook more uniformly than irregularly shaped foods.

MICROWAVE COOKING TECHNIQUES

When cooking conventionally there are a few rules to follow; the same is true for microwave cooking. By observing a few simple guide lines, you can count on good results.

Timing is extremely important. Two to three minutes of extra cooking will dehydrate and toughen many foods. It is a good idea to check the timer on your oven occasionally with another clock when cooking, to see if the timer is accurate. The recipe cooking times in this book are for 600- to 650-watt ovens. If using an oven with a lower wattage, increase the timing as necessary.

Rotating, stirring, and turning are necessary for even distribution of the microwave energy. The cooking pattern in foods cooked in microwave ovens tends to be circular, with a hole in the middle, somewhat like a doughnut. The center of a dish receives the least amount of the microwaves and hence is slower to cook. To minimize this problem, when baking cakes, meat loaves, puddings, etc., it is often recommended that a glass be placed right side up in the center of the dish so no uncooked spot is in the center.

When cooking only one dish in the oven, rotating the dish one-quarter or one-half turn is sufficient to expose the food to an even distribution of energy. Rotating is also necessary when more than one item is being cooked at the same time. For example, if six cupcakes in glass custard cups are baking in the oven, they should be arranged in a ring and their position changed during the cooking time. The individual cupcakes are not rotated, but the circle of cupcakes is turned for a better distribution of energy. Because of the "doughnut" effect of heat patterns, it is advised that foods be arranged in a circle whenever possible. Turning foods over is sometimes necessary. When cooking foods of different sizes and shapes, place the large, thick, dense pieces near the edge of the baking dish and the smaller pieces near the center. When a soup, sauce, or beverage is being heated, it should be stirred to distribute the heat and warm the liquid more rapidly.

Cover foods in the microwave oven as you would cover conventionally cooked foods. Covers are used to trap steam and moisture and to increase the heat, making a softer, more tender product. Roasts and most casseroles are not covered, but vegetables should always be covered. Some foods, such as potatoes, provide their own covering—their skins. These skins need to be pierced prior to baking so they do not burst from the accumulated steam inside. An inverted plate or piece of waxed paper may be used to cover a dish without a lid. If using plastic wrap, be careful not be burn yourself from accumulated steam when removing the plastic wrap from the dish. Always follow the covering instructions given with each recipe.

"Shielding" is a term applied to the placing of small pieces of aluminum foil on parts of a piece of meat or baked product that require less microwave energy. The metal reflects the microwaves, so additional cooking does not occur in that area. Aluminum foil should never touch the sides of the oven cavity.

Carry-over cooking time is required for almost every item cooked in the microwave. This is a few minutes in which the food is resting after being cooked to allow it to finish cooking. Allow large items (roasts and casseroles) to rest 10 to 15 minutes; medium-sized items (vegetables), 5 to 10 minutes; and small foods or little amounts of food (eggs or bread), 1 or 2 minutes. Always allow the food to finish its carry-over cooking before returning it to the microwave for additional cooking if it does not look done when removed from the oven. It is surprising how much cooking occurs during this carry-over time.

Browning will generally occur naturally with most meats and large dishes cooked 10 to 15 minutes or more in the microwave oven. If additional browning is desired, the food, in a metal or glass ceramic container, may be placed under a hot conventional broiler for a few minutes. Some foods may also be browned on top of a conventional range and the cooking finished in a microwave oven.

A grilled, seared, or broiled effect may be achieved by using a ceramic browning dish designed especially for microwave oven use, which may be purchased from a microwave dealer. Browning dishes are used as a fry pan would be used on the range to grill both sides of the food.

Baked products cook in such a short time, because of their porous structure, that they do not develop surface browning. You can improve appearance of these products, if you wish, by frosting the cakes or cupcakes, sprinkling cinnamon or nuts on muffins and quick breads, or adding a dark sauce or crumb topping to a casserole.

Defrosting can be done in the microwave oven by allowing 2 minutes per pound heating time for each pound of frozen food. When defrosting food, it must also be rotated and shielded as needed. If the food is defrosted on the "high" setting, a carry-over cooking time is needed at the end of the heating time. If the defrost cycle is used, the resting time is allowed for during the heating time, but the oven often requires 4 minutes per pound defrosting time. Always defrost food completely before cooking, and consult your oven manual for specifics about your defrost unit.

Slow-cooking, or reducing the amount of energy in the oven, is done by using the defrost setting as the medium setting on a conventional range would be used. As the amount of energy is reduced, the cooking time increases accordingly. On the defrost setting for slow cooking, the cooking time normally required at high would have to be doubled. If your oven has *variable speeds,* adjust the amount of energy as you would adjust the heat on a conventional range, from high to medium high,

to medium, to medium low, to low. Approximately 95 percent of your cooking will be done on high. You may want to reduce the energy when cooking foods that have a tendency to boil over, such as scalloped potatoes.

Foods cooked in a microwave oven will not always be the same as foods cooked conventionally. Baked potatoes are more fluffy and light and the skin does not dry as it does in a conventional oven. Casseroles do not dry out on the surface when reheated. Cakes are very tender and light, provided they are not overcooked. Sauces with a high sugar content are more grainy than those cooked conventionally. Vegetables turn out crisp-tender, similar to Oriental-style vegetables.

APPETIZERS AND SNACKS

The microwave is great for entertaining and super for serving appetizers and snacks. They may be made ahead and frozen for reheating as needed, or they can be prepared and heated as needed to serve a crowd.

The arrangement of food on the plate is important in cooking appetizers, and the plate must be rotated halfway through cooking. If they have been cooked, only a reheating time is needed.

Appetizers using a bread or cracker base should be combined at the last minute to prevent the cracker from absorbing moisture from the filling. You can also let your guests fix their own appetizers. Friends are all very curious about how the microwave works, anyway!

We always keep on hand for guests the ingredients for a quick "dip" that can be heated rapidly in the microwave at a moment's notice.

Seafood Crackers

1 can (8 ounces) crab or shrimp, drained, or 1½ pounds cooked fresh fish
1 tablespoon sliced green onion
1 cup shredded Swiss cheese
½ cup mayonnaise
1 teaspoon lemon juice
25 crisp crackers

1. In a 1-quart mixing bowl, combine seafood, onion, cheese, mayonnaise, and lemon juice.
2. Spread 1 teaspoon filling on each cracker. Arrange 10 to 12 crackers in a circle on glass plate or waxed paper.
3. Cook 45 seconds to 1 minute, rotating dish one-quarter turn halfway through cooking time. Serve hot.

25 appetizers

Sweet-and-Sour Wiener Fondue

1 jar (5 ounces) currant jelly
½ cup prepared mustard
1 pound wieners, cut in bite-size pieces

1. In a small glass mixing bowl, combine jelly and mustard. Cook 2 minutes, stirring halfway through cooking time.
2. Add wieners and cook 3 to 4 minutes, stirring halfway through cooking time.
3. Serve warm.

60 to 70 appetizers

Stuffed Mushrooms

1 **bunch green onions, chopped**
¼ **cup dairy sour cream**
½ **teaspoon Worcestershire sauce**
½ **teaspoon oregano**
½ **cup bulk pork sausage**
1 **pound fresh mushrooms, washed, drained, and stemmed**

1. In a 1-quart glass casserole, blend green onions, sour cream, Worcestershire sauce, oregano, and sausage. Cook 2 to 3 minutes, stirring halfway through cooking time.
2. Stuff mushroom caps with filling. Place stem in top of filling and secure in place with wooden pick.
3. Arrange 10 to 12 mushrooms evenly around the edge of a glass pie plate and cook, covered, 6 to 8 minutes.
4. Serve warm.

25 to 30 appetizers

Greek Meatballs

1 **pound ground lamb**
1 **egg**
⅓ **cup cracker crumbs**
⅓ **cup soy sauce**
½ **cup water**
¼ **teaspoon ginger**
¼ **teaspoon garlic powder**
⅛ **teaspoon cumin**
½ **cup pinenuts or slivered almonds**

1. In a medium mixing bowl, blend lamb, egg, and cracker crumbs. Add soy sauce, water, ginger, garlic powder, cumin, and pinenuts. Mix thoroughly. Shape in 1-inch meatballs.
2. Arrange 10 meatballs in a circle in a 9-inch glass pie plate. Cook, covered, 3 to 4 minutes, rotating dish one-quarter turn halfway through cooking time. Cook longer if needed.
3. Serve hot on wooden picks.

50 to 60 meatballs

Chicken-Stuffed Mushrooms

30 **fresh medium mushrooms**
1 **can (4¾ ounces) chicken spread**
½ **teaspoon seasoned salt**
⅛ **teaspoon pepper**
1 **tablespoon chopped parsley**
½ **cup chopped walnuts**

1. Wash mushrooms quickly under cold water. Remove stems, and drain both stems and caps on paper towel.
2. In a small mixing bowl, blend chicken spread, seasoned salt, pepper, parsley, and walnuts. Stuff mushrooms; place stems in filling and secure with wooden pick.
3. Arrange mushrooms on a glass pie plate and cook, covered with waxed paper, 6 to 8 minutes, rotating dish one-quarter turn halfway through cooking time. Serve hot.

30 appetizers

Conventional oven: Bake at 350°F 20 minutes.

Spicy Beef Dip

1 **pound ground beef**
½ **cup chopped onion**
1 **clove garlic, minced**
1 **can (8 ounces) tomato sauce**
¼ **cup ketchup**
¾ **teaspoon oregano, crushed**
1 **teaspoon sugar**
1 **package (3 ounces) cream cheese**
⅓ **cup grated Parmesan cheese**

1. In a 1½-quart glass casserole, sauté ground beef, onion, and garlic 4 to 6 minutes, stirring twice.
2. Spoon off excess fat. Stir in tomato sauce, ketchup, oregano, and sugar.
3. Cover and cook 5 to 6 minutes, stirring twice.
4. Add cream cheese and Parmesan cheese, and stir until cream cheese has melted. Serve warm.

About 3 cups dip

Appetizer Kabobs

8 large precooked smoked sausage
   links
1 can (16 ounces) pineapple chunks,
   drained
1 tablespoon brown sugar
2 tablespoons soy sauce
1 tablespoon vinegar

1. Arrange sausage evenly around edge of roasting rack set in a glass dish or directly on glass plate and cook 2 to 3 minutes, rotating dish one-quarter turn halfway through cooking time. Drain sausage and cut each sausage link into 5 pieces.
2. Make kabobs, using 1 sausage piece and 1 pineapple chunk threaded on a round wooden pick. Arrange evenly in a large shallow dish.
3. In a 1-cup glass measure, blend brown sugar, soy sauce, and vinegar and pour over kabobs. Refrigerate 1 or 2 hours until serving time.
4. Arrange 20 kabobs on a large glass plate and cook 2 to 3 minutes, rotating dish one-quarter turn and spooning sauce over top halfway through cooking time.
5. Cook additional kabobs as needed. Serve warm.

40 appetizers

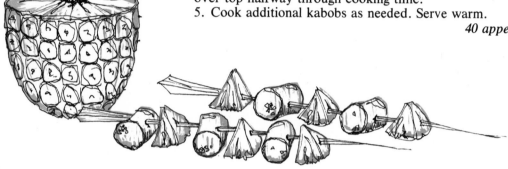

Snackin' Nuts

¼ cup sugar
½ teaspoon cinnamon
1 tablespoon brown sugar
2 tablespoons butter
2 cups pecan halves

1. Combine sugar, cinnamon, and brown sugar; set aside.
2. In a 2-quart glass casserole, heat butter 30 seconds. Add nuts and cook 4 to 5 minutes, stirring every minute.
3. Add sugar mixture to nuts and stir to coat nuts evenly. Spread out on wooden board to cool.
4. Serve warm or cold.

2 cups nuts

Note: May be stored in freezer.

Super Snack

6 cups puffed rice cereal
4 cups pretzel sticks
1 box (10 ounces) puffed oat circles
1 can (7 ounces) salted peanuts
½ cup butter
2 teaspoons Worcestershire sauce
½ teaspoon paprika
1 teaspoon dry mustard
1 teaspoon onion salt
1 teaspoon garlic powder

1. In a large glass bowl, combine rice cereal, pretzel sticks, oat circles, and peanuts.
2. In a 2-cup glass measure, combine butter, Worcestershire sauce, paprika, mustard, onion salt, and garlic powder. Cook 1 to 1½ minutes until butter is melted; stir to blend evenly. Pour over dry ingredients.
3. Cook 5 to 7 minutes, stirring to mix ingredients every 2 minutes.
4. Cool before serving. Store in airtight container.

About 6 quarts

Note: Snack mixture may be frozen, then reheated before serving.

Swedish Meatballs

1 **pound ground beef**
¼ **cup dry bread crumbs**
¼ **cup minced onion**
2 **tablespoons chopped parsley**
½ **teaspoon salt**
1 **teaspoon sugar**
½ **teaspoon allspice**
¼ **teaspoon nutmeg**
1 **egg, lightly beaten**
1 **can (10½ ounces) condensed cream of celery soup**
½ **soup can water**
2 **tablespoons minced dill pickle**

1. In a mixing bowl, combine ground beef, bread crumbs, onion, parsley, salt, sugar, allspice, nutmeg, and egg. Mix well and form into 24 meatballs.
2. Arrange meatballs in a circle on roasting rack placed in a 2-quart baking dish. Cover with waxed paper and cook 5 to 7 minutes, rotating dish one-quarter turn halfway through cooking.
3. Remove rack and meatballs from dish. Pour off drippings and return meatballs to dish.
4. In a 2-cup measure, blend soup, water, and pickle; pour over meatballs.
5. Cook, covered, 4 to 6 minutes, stirring halfway through cooking time.
6. Rest 10 minutes before serving.

24 appetizers

Conventional range: Simmer over low heat 20 to 25 minutes.

Pumpkin Seeds

1 **cup raw pumpkin seeds**
  Salt

1. Rinse fibers from seeds and pat seeds dry with paper towel.
2. Sprinkle seeds with a light, even coating of salt.
3. In a glass pie plate, arrange seeds in a single layer.
4. Cook 6 to 7 minutes, stirring every minute, until seeds are crisp.
5. Rub seeds between fingers to remove excess salt.

1 cup seeds

Winter Squash Seeds: Follow directions for Pumpkin Seeds, substituting **1 cup winter squash seeds.**

Sunflower Seeds: Follow directions for Pumpkin Seeds, substituting **1 cup hulled sunflower seeds.** Cook 4 to 5 minutes, stirring every minute, until crisp.

SOUPS AND SAUCES

Small or individual portions of soup, in serving bowls or mugs, generally heat best in the microwave. For cooking larger quantities, select a deep container; if covered, the soup will cook in less time. Stirring may be necessary several times during the heating or cooking to distribute the heat evenly in the container. If you hear an eruption while your soup is cooking, the liquid is getting close to the boiling stage and the mixture needs stirring to distribute the heat.

Many soups we prefer to cook conventionally to improve the flavor. They can also be prepared in advance, and the flavor will improve with standing. Reheat in the microwave as desired.

The microwave almost makes sauces a convenience food. They are cooked very quickly in a glass measuring cup, which is the ideal container to use. The wooden spoon can be left in the container for stirring, which is often necessary.

Sauces which have a flour or cornstarch base must be boiled to thicken. When eggs are the base, the sauce will need stirring more often to prevent cooking the outer edges of the sauce and making it curdle.

Mock Bouillabaisse

1 small onion, sliced
1 clove garlic, minced
1 bay leaf
¼ teaspoon thyme
2 tablespoons olive oil
1 can (10¾ ounces) condensed
    tomato soup
¾ soup can water
2 cups cooked seafood
1 teaspoon lemon juice
    Dash Tabasco
3 or 4 slices French bread, toasted

1. In a 3-quart glass casserole, combine onion, garlic, bay leaf, thyme, and olive oil. Cook 3 to 4 minutes, stirring halfway through cooking time, until onion is tender.
2. Stir in soup, water, seafood, lemon juice, and Tabasco.
3. Heat 6 to 8 minutes, stirring every 2 minutes, until boiling.
4. Cover and cook an additional 2 minutes.
5. Rest 5 minutes. Ladle soup over toast in bowls.

3 or 4 servings

Tomato-Leek Soup

2 tablespoons butter
2 leeks, chopped (about 2½ cups)
2 carrots, finely diced (about 1 cup)
2 tablespoons flour
2 beef bouillon cubes
2 cups boiling water
1 to 2 teaspoons sugar
¼ teaspoon salt
4 large ripe tomatoes (2 pounds), peeled and cut in pieces

1. Heat butter in a 2½-quart glass bowl about 30 seconds. Add leeks and carrots and heat 4 to 5 minutes, stirring halfway through cooking.
2. Stir in flour and heat 1 to 1½ minutes.
3. Dissolve bouillon cubes in water and stir into the vegetables. Bring to boiling, about 2½ to 3 minutes, stirring after every minute. Continue cooking 4 minutes, stirring after 2 minutes.
4. Stir in sugar, salt, and tomatoes. Heat 20 to 25 minutes, stirring every 5 minutes, until tomatoes are soft.

4 servings

Creamed Onion Soup

4 medium onions, sliced
½ cup butter
¼ cup flour
1 quart milk
2 cups chicken broth or 2 chicken bouillon cubes dissolved in 2 cups boiling water
1 to 1½ teaspoons salt
1 egg yolk
1 tablespoon minced parsley
½ cup croutons

1. In a 3-quart glass casserole, sauté onions in butter 4 to 5 minutes, stirring every minute. Stir in flour and cook until sauce bubbles, about 1 minute.
2. Add milk slowly, stirring gently. Cook until slightly thickened, about 6 to 8 minutes, stirring every 2 minutes.
3. Add broth and cook 5 minutes, stirring twice.
4. Stir in salt to taste. Blend some of the hot soup with egg yolk and return to remaining soup. Cook 1 minute, stirring every 15 seconds.
5. Serve topped with minced parsley and croutons.

8 servings

Clam Chowder (Manhattan Style)

4 slices bacon
1 can (8 ounces) minced clams
2 medium potatoes, pared and cubed
¼ cup chopped onion
1 can (16 ounces) whole tomatoes (undrained)
2 tablespoons flour
1 teaspoon salt
¼ teaspoon pepper
½ teaspoon oregano

1. Arrange bacon on the rack in a 2-quart glass baking dish. Cook 2 to 3 minutes, rotating dish one-quarter turn halfway through cooking time. Lift rack from dish; set bacon aside.
2. Drain clams, reserving liquor. Add clam liquor, potatoes, onion, and tomatoes to drippings in dish and cook, covered, 10 to 12 minutes, stirring halfway through cooking time.
3. Blend flour with ¼ cup hot liquid from dish. Stir salt, pepper, oregano, and clams into flour mixture. Add to liquid in dish, blending well. Cook, covered, 5 to 6 minutes or until mixture boils, stirring every 2 minutes.
4. Rest, covered, 5 minutes before serving. Garnish with cooked bacon.

4 servings

Microwave Cooking Utensils and Containers, 8

Clam-and-Corn Chowder

4 slices bacon, cooked (page 38)
1 small onion, thinly sliced
1 can (16 ounces) New England-style
   clam chowder
2 cups milk
1 can (12 ounces) corn, drained
¼ teaspoon thyme
½ teaspoon salt
¼ teaspoon pepper

1. When bacon is cold, crumble in bits; set aside.
2. Sauté onion in bacon drippings 2 to 3 minutes; set aside.
3. In a 2-quart glass casserole, combine clam chowder, milk, corn, and thyme. Stir in onion.
4. Cook 4 to 5 minutes, stirring every minute, until mixture steams. Stir in salt and pepper.
5. Serve garnished with bacon bits.

4 to 6 servings

Meatless Spaghetti Sauce

2 tablespoons salad oil
1 medium onion, minced
1 can (28 ounces) whole tomatoes
   (undrained)
1 can (6 ounces) tomato paste
½ teaspoon garlic powder
1 tablespoon chopped fresh parsley
½ teaspoon oregano
½ teaspoon salt
¼ teaspoon pepper
½ teaspoon sugar

1. In a 2-quart glass casserole, heat oil 30 seconds. Stir in onion and cook 3 to 4 minutes, stirring halfway through cooking time.
2. Add tomatoes, tomato paste, garlic powder, parsley, oregano, salt, pepper, and sugar. Stir to blend.
3. Cook 15 to 20 minutes, stirring every 5 minutes.
4. Serve over cooked **spaghetti.**

6 to 8 servings

Spaghetti Meat Sauce

1 pound ground beef
1 clove garlic, minced
1 small onion, chopped
1 can (15 ounces) tomato sauce
1 teaspoon oregano
½ teaspoon basil
½ teaspoon salt
¼ teaspoon pepper
½ cup tomato juice or ketchup

1. In a 2-quart glass casserole, brown ground beef 2 to 3 minutes, stirring to crumble.
2. Stir in garlic and onion. Cook, covered, 5 minutes, stirring halfway through cooking time.
3. Add tomato sauce, oregano, basil, salt, pepper, and tomato juice.
4. Cook, covered, 15 to 20 minutes, stirring several times. Rest, covered, 5 minutes.
5. Serve over **cooked spaghetti,** and sprinkle with **grated Parmesan cheese.**

4 servings

Gravy

¼ cup flour
¼ cup drippings
2 cups broth, water, or milk
1 teaspoon salt
¼ teaspoon pepper

1. In a 4-cup glass measure, blend flour into drippings to make a smooth paste. Gradually stir in liquid until smooth.
2. Cook 1 to 3 minutes, stirring every minute, until smooth and thickened. Add salt and pepper; stir to blend.
3. Cook 30 seconds to 1 minute.

2 cups

Greek Meatballs, 12;
Appetizer Kabobs, 13;
Chicken-Stuffed Mushrooms, 12

Foolproof Hollandaise Sauce

¼ **cup butter**
¼ **teaspoon salt**
½ **teaspoon dry mustard**
2 **egg yolks, beaten**
¼ **cup milk or cream**
1 **tablespoon lemon juice**

1. In a 2-cup glass measure, heat butter 30 seconds. Add salt, dry mustard, egg yolks, milk, and lemon juice; stir to blend evenly.
2. Cook 1 to 1½ minutes, stirring every 15 seconds. Beat with a wire whisk until smooth and light.

⅔ cup

Barbecue Sauce

½ **cup diced onion**
¼ **cup diced green pepper**
2 **cans (6 ounces each) tomato paste**
½ **teaspoon dry mustard**
⅓ **cup vinegar**
1 **can (15¼ ounces) crushed pineapple (undrained)**
¼ **cup brown sugar**

1. In a 4-cup glass measure, cook onion and green pepper 1½ minutes, stirring once halfway through cooking time. Add tomato paste, mustard, vinegar, pineapple, and brown sugar. Stir to blend.
2. Cook 2 to 3 minutes, stirring halfway through cooking time.

About 3½ cups

Medium White Sauce

2 **tablespoons butter**
2 **tablespoons flour**
½ **teaspoon salt**
1 **cup milk**

1. In a 2-cup glass measure, heat butter 30 seconds. Stir in flour and salt, blending until smooth.
2. Add milk gradually, stirring to blend.
3. Cook 2 to 3 minutes, stirring every minute, until thickened.

1 cup

Thin White Sauce: Follow recipe for Medium White Sauce. Use 1 tablespoon butter and 1 tablespoon flour.

Thick White Sauce: Follow recipe for Medium White Sauce. Use 3 to 4 tablespoons butter and 3 to 4 tablespoons flour.

Cheese Sauce: Follow recipe for Medium White Sauce. When sauce is thickened, add ¾ **cup shredded sharp Cheddar cheese,** ¼ **teaspoon dry mustard,** and **dash paprika;** blend well. Cook 1 minute and stir to blend.

Cranberry Sauce

2 **cups sugar**
1 **cup water**
1 **pound fresh cranberries (4 cups)**

1. Dissolve sugar in water in a 3-quart glass casserole. Stir in cranberries and cover dish.
2. Cook 8 to 10 minutes, stirring every 3 or 4 minutes, or until mixture boils and cranberries begin to pop.
3. Rest 10 minutes. Serve warm or chilled.

About 4 cups sauce

BREADS, SANDWICHES, AND CEREALS

Because of their porous texture most bread products require little cooking time. When overcooked, they will become dry and tough. It is best when in doubt to undercook, and add to the cooking time as needed. Foods with a combination of densities and chemical properties, such as sweet rolls, will require even less cooking time. Heat rolls and breads on a paper towel to absorb moisture, or on a roasting rack. If placed directly on a glass container, the moisture will condense on the container, making the bottom soggy.

Cereals have a tendency to boil over, so it is important to select a dish large enough to allow for this boiling. Also, stir several times during the cooking to distribute the heat evenly.

Hot sandwiches are a breeze to make in the microwave oven—generally 45 to 60 seconds is all that is required for heating one sandwich. Use day-old bread; it heats better than fresh bread. Or if you prefer a toasted sandwich, toast the bread before making the sandwich.

We find that sandwiches heat more evenly when placed on a roasting rack, paper towel, or napkin. We also prefer to slice the sandwich and arrange with the center portion toward the outside edge of the plate, since the bulk of the filling is in this area.

Pumpkin Bread

1½ **cups sugar**
⅓ **cup salad oil**
2 **eggs**
1 **cup canned pumpkin**
1½ **cups all-purpose flour**
¾ **teaspoon salt**
½ **teaspoon cinnamon**
½ **teaspoon nutmeg**
½ **teaspoon cloves**
½ **teaspoon allspice**
1 **teaspoon baking soda**
¼ **teaspoon baking powder**
½ **cup coarsely chopped walnuts**

1. In a large mixing bowl, blend sugar, oil, eggs, and pumpkin. When ingredients are well mixed, stir in flour, salt, cinnamon, nutmeg, cloves, allspice, baking soda, and baking powder, blending well. Stir in walnuts. Pour batter into an 8×4-inch glass dish.
2. Cook 12 to 14 minutes, rotating dish one-quarter turn every 4 minutes. Knife inserted in the center should come out clean when bread is done.
3. Rest 5 minutes and remove from pan. Serve either warm or cold with **butter** or **cream cheese.**

1 loaf bread

Quick Cheese Bread

2½ cups all-purpose biscuit mix
1 cup shredded sharp Cheddar
cheese
1 tablespoon poppy seed
1 egg
1 cup milk

1. In a medium mixing bowl, blend biscuit mix, cheese, poppy seed, egg, and milk. Stir just to moisten. Pour into a buttered 8-inch square glass baking dish.
2. Cook 5 to 7 minutes, rotating dish one-quarter turn halfway through cooking time. Allow to stand 5 minutes. Center will be soft but will set with standing.

9 to 12 servings

Note: A glass may be placed in the center of dish before pouring in batter to help the bread cook. A 9-inch round glass baking dish may also be used.

The bread may be browned under a conventional broiler for 1 to 2 minutes, but only if a glass ceramic baking dish is used, or the bread is transferred to a metal pan.

Quick Cheese Muffins: Follow recipe for Quick Cheese Bread. Line custard cups, paper drinking cups, or cupcaker with paper baking cups. Fill each cup half full with batter. Arrange 6 cups in a circle in microwave oven. Bake for 2 to 2½ minutes, rearranging cups halfway through cooking time.

About 1½ dozen muffins

Assorted Hot Rolls

The microwave oven is a real aid in serving piping hot rolls at every meal. Heating times may vary, depending on whether the roll has a filling, icing, or nut coating. Always undercook rolls rather than overcook them. Any complaints about dry, tough rolls are always an indication of overcooking.

Rolls (plain or sweet)

1. Place rolls in a napkin, terry towel, or napkin in a wooden bread basket.
2. Heat as follows: 1 roll, 10 to 15 seconds; 2 rolls, 20 to 30 seconds; 4 rolls, 40 to 60 seconds; and 6 rolls, 1 to 1¼ minutes. Always start with the shortest time, and heat longer if necessary.
3. Serve immediately while warm.

Peanut Butter Coffee Cake

2 cups all-purpose biscuit mix
2 tablespoons sugar
¼ cup peanut butter, chunky or
smooth
⅔ cup milk
1 egg
½ cup jelly or jam (optional)

1. Combine biscuit mix and sugar; cut in peanut butter with a fork. Stir in milk and egg; blend evenly. Pour into a buttered 9-inch glass dish. Swirl jelly through batter, if desired.
2. Cook 8 to 10 minutes, rotating dish one-quarter turn halfway through cooking time.
3. Rest 5 minutes before serving.

4 to 6 servings

Coffee Cake Ring

½ cup butter
¾ cup brown sugar
1 egg
1 cup whole wheat pancake mix
1 teaspoon vanilla extract
¼ cup water
1 cup quick-cooking oats
½ cup butterscotch-flavored pieces
½ cup chopped walnuts

1. In a mixing bowl, blend butter, brown sugar, egg, and pancake mix.
2. Add vanilla extract, water, oats, butterscotch-flavored pieces, and walnuts. Stir until evenly blended.
3. Place small glass, open end up, in center of 8-inch glass dish. Pour batter into dish around glass.
4. Cook 4 to 6 minutes, rotating dish one-quarter turn halfway through cooking time. Rest 5 minutes.
5. Serve warm.

6 to 8 servings

Muffin Bread

5 cups all-purpose flour
2 packages active dry yeast
1 tablespoon sugar
2 teaspoons salt
2½ cups milk
½ teaspoon baking soda
1 tablespoon warm water
¼ cup cornmeal

1. In a large bowl, blend 3 cups flour, yeast, sugar, and salt.
2. In a 4-cup glass measure, heat milk 2 to 3 minutes until warm.
3. Stir milk into flour mixture and blend well. Stir in remaining flour. Cover; let rise in a warm place until doubled, about 1 hour.
4. Blend baking soda and water, then stir into batter, blending well. Divide batter in half; place in two 8×4-inch loaf dishes. Cover; let rise until doubled, about 1 hour.
5. Sprinkle 2 tablespoons cornmeal on top of each loaf.
6. Cook loaves individually 5 to 6 minutes, rotating dish one-quarter turn every 2 minutes.
7. Rest 5 minutes and remove from dish.
8. Slice and toast before serving.

2 loaves bread

Sour Cream Coffee Cake

½ cup butter
1 cup sugar
3 eggs
1 teaspoon vanilla extract
1 cup dairy sour cream
2 cups all-purpose flour
1 teaspoon baking powder
1 teaspoon baking soda
¾ cup firmly packed brown sugar
¼ cup butter
¼ cup all-purpose flour
¼ teaspoon salt
¼ teaspoon cinnamon
1 cup chopped walnuts

1. In a mixing bowl, cream butter and sugar. Add eggs and stir to blend. Stir in vanilla extract and sour cream. Add flour, baking powder, and baking soda. Stir until well mixed.
2. Line bottom of two 8-inch round glass baking dishes with waxed paper. Pour one quarter of the batter into each cake pan.
3. In a small mixing bowl, combine brown sugar, butter, flour, salt, and cinnamon; stir until crumbly. Mix in nuts.
4. Sprinkle one quarter of the nut mixture on each cake layer. Divide remaining batter between each dish, and pour over nut mixture. Cover with remaining nut mixture.
5. Cook 1 dish at a time, covered with waxed paper, 4 to 5 minutes, rotating dish one-quarter turn halfway through cooking time.
6. Rest 5 minutes before serving.

12 to 16 servings

Note: Cooked coffee cake may be frozen.

Blueberry Streusel

1½ cups all-purpose flour
¾ cup uncooked oats
1 cup firmly packed brown sugar
½ teaspoon baking soda
½ teaspoon salt
½ cup butter
1 can (21 ounces) blueberry pie filling

1. In a large mixing bowl, blend flour, oats, brown sugar, baking soda, and salt. Cut butter into dry mixture until crumbly. Spread one half of mixture into an 8-inch glass baking dish, and press firmly in bottom.
2. Spread pie filling evenly over crumb mixture. Top pie filling with remaining crumb mixture.
3. Cook 12 to 15 minutes, rotating dish one-quarter turn halfway through cooking time.
4. Serve warm or cold.

8 or 9 servings

Note: Any fruit pie filling may be used.

Raisin Bran Muffins

½ cup sugar
⅓ cup shortening
1 egg
1 cup all-purpose flour
2 teaspoons baking powder
½ teaspoon baking soda
½ teaspoon salt
2 cups raisin bran flakes
1 cup buttermilk

1. In a medium mixing bowl, cream sugar and shortening. Add egg and beat until light and fluffy.
2. Add flour, baking powder, baking soda, and salt; stir to blend. Fold in raisin bran flakes and buttermilk. Stir just to moisten.
3. Line custard cups, paper drinking cups, or cupcaker with paper cups. Fill each cup no more than half full. Arrange 6 cups in a circle and cook 3 to 3½ minutes, rearranging cups halfway through cooking time.
4. Serve warm with **butter** and **jelly.**

12 to 14 muffins

Cheese Rolls

8 hot dog buns or French rolls
Soft butter
½ cup grated Parmesan cheese
⅓ cup poppy seed

1. Slice each roll in half lengthwise. Spread all cut sides with soft butter.
2. In a glass pie plate, mix cheese and poppy seed. Press buttered sides of each roll in cheese mixture.
3. Wrap 4 rolls in paper towel, napkin, or terry towel and cook 45 seconds to 1 minute. Repeat procedure with remaining 4 rolls.

8 cheese rolls

Conventional oven: Bake at 350°F 10 to 12 minutes.

Note: Rolls may be cut smaller and served with salad or soup. Cheese rolls may be placed under the broiler 1 minute for crisping before serving.

Cheese and Bacon Sandwiches

12 slices wheat bread, toasted
6 slices process American cheese
12 slices bacon, cooked and cut in
    half
6 slices Swiss cheese

1. On each of 6 toast slices, place 1 slice American cheese, 4 bacon halves, and 1 slice Swiss cheese. Top with remaining pieces of toast.
2. Cook as follows, rotating one-quarter turn halfway through cooking time: 45 to 60 seconds for 1 sandwich; 2 to 2½ minutes for 3 sandwiches; and 3 to 4 minutes for 6 sandwiches.
3. Serve warm.

6 sandwiches

Frankfurter Reuben

12 slices rye bread
    Butter
6 large frankfurters
⅓ cup Thousand Island dressing
1 cup sauerkraut, well drained
6 slices Swiss cheese

1. Toast bread, and butter each piece on 1 side. Split frankfurters in half lengthwise and place on buttered side of 6 slices toast. Spread dressing on frankfurters, and top each sandwich with about 2 tablespoons sauerkraut. Place 1 slice cheese on each sandwich. Top each with slice of remaining bread, buttered side towards cheese.
2. Cook as follows, rotating one-quarter turn halfway through cooking time: 45 to 60 seconds for 1 sandwich; 2 to 2½ minutes for 3 sandwiches; and 3 to 4 minutes for 6 sandwiches.
3. Serve warm.

6 sandwiches

Chili Burgers

2 pounds ground beef
1 medium onion, diced
1¼ cups diced celery
3 tablespoons vinegar
1 bottle (14 ounces) ketchup
1 can (8 ounces) tomato sauce
2 tablespoons dry mustard
½ cup water
¼ cup Worcestershire sauce
1½ teaspoons salt
½ teaspoon pepper
½ teaspoon chili powder
8 hamburger buns

1. In a 3-quart glass casserole, sauté ground beef, onion, and celery 6 to 8 minutes, stirring every 2 minutes. Drain off drippings.
2. Add vinegar, ketchup, tomato sauce, mustard, water, Worcestershire sauce, salt, pepper, and chili powder; stir to blend ingredients evenly.
3. Cook, covered, 8 to 10 minutes.
4. Heat buns wrapped in terry towel 1 to 1½ minutes.
5. Spoon mixture on heated buns.

6 to 8 servings

Conventional oven: Bake at 350°F 1½ hours.

Note: This is a good mixture to make ahead and keep frozen.

Tortilla Sandwiches

12 corn tortillas
    Salad oil
6 slices Monterey Jack cheese

1. Fry tortillas in small amount of hot oil on range until limp. Fold in half and hold slightly open with tongs; continue to fry until crisp, turning to fry on both sides. Drain on paper towel.
2. Place ½ slice cheese in each tortilla. Arrange tortillas in shallow glass dish in microwave and cook 1 to 1½ minutes, rotating dish one-quarter turn halfway through cooking time.
3. Serve hot; reheat if needed.

12 sandwiches

Stromboli Sandwich

1 pound ground beef
2 tablespoons finely chopped onion
½ cup tomato sauce
½ cup ketchup
2 tablespoons grated Parmesan
   cheese
½ teaspoon garlic salt
¼ teaspoon oregano
½ teaspoon garlic powder
¼ cup butter
6 French rolls
6 slices mozzarella cheese

1. In a 1½-quart glass casserole, combine ground beef and onion. Cook 4 to 5 minutes, stirring halfway through cooking time. Spoon off drippings.
2. Stir in tomato sauce, ketchup, Parmesan cheese, garlic salt, and oregano. Cook, covered, 5 to 6 minutes, stirring halfway through cooking time.
3. In a 1-cup glass measure, combine garlic powder and butter; heat 30 seconds. Stir to blend. Pour melted butter evenly over inside of top half of each roll.
4. Divide meat mixture evenly and spread on bottom halves of each roll. Top with 1 slice mozzarella, place tops on buns, and wrap each in a napkin.
5. Cook as follows, rotating one-quarter turn halfway through cooking time: 30 to 45 seconds for 1 sandwich; 1½ to 2 minutes for 3 sandwiches; and 3 to 4 minutes for 6 sandwiches.
6. Serve warm.

6 sandwiches

Confetti Rice

1½ cups water
1 teaspoon salt
2 cups butter
1½ cups packaged precooked rice
2 tablespoons finely chopped
   pimento
2 tablespoons minced parsley

1. In a 1-quart glass casserole, combine water, salt, and butter.
2. Cook, covered, 3 to 4 minutes, or until water boils. Stir in rice, cover, and rest 5 to 7 minutes.
3. Stir in pimento and parsley just before serving.

4 servings

Beefy Rice

1 beef bouillon cube
1¾ cups water
1 cup uncooked white rice
½ cup butter
1 teaspoon salt
1 tablespoon parsley flakes

1. In a 3-quart glass casserole, combine bouillon cube, water, rice, butter, and salt.
2. Cook, covered, 12 to 14 minutes, stirring halfway through cooking time.
3. Rest, covered, 10 minutes. Stir in parsley flakes.

4 to 6 servings

Conventional oven: Bake at 375°F 1 hour.

Long Grain Rice

2½ cups water
1 cup long grain rice
1 teaspoon salt

1. In a covered 2-quart glass casserole, bring water to boiling, 5 to 6 minutes. Stir in rice and salt.
2. Cook, covered, 7 to 9 minutes, rotating dish one-quarter turn halfway through cooking time.
3. Rest, covered, 10 minutes before serving.

5 or 6 servings

Cheesy Rice Casserole

1 envelope (1½ ounces) dry onion
    soup mix
1½ cups packaged precooked rice
1 can (10½ ounces) condensed
    Cheddar cheese soup
1⅓ cups milk

1. In a 2-quart glass casserole, sprinkle onion soup mix evenly over bottom of casserole. Sprinkle rice over soup mix.
2. Blend cheese soup with milk. Pour over rice, stirring to blend lightly.
3. Cook, covered, 10 to 12 minutes, rotating dish one-quarter turn halfway through cooking time.
4. Rest, covered, 5 minutes before serving.

4 to 6 servings

Variation: **2 to 3 chicken breasts,** cut in half, or **1 pound fresh white fish,** cut in serving pieces, may be placed on top of rice before cooking. Sprinkle with **paprika** and cook, covered, 20 minutes for chicken, and 15 minutes for fish.

Green Rice Casserole

3 cups cooked rice (page 24)
¼ cup finely chopped green pepper
1 cup finely chopped parsley
½ cup (2 ounces) shredded sharp
    Cheddar cheese
¼ cup finely chopped onion
1 teaspoon salt
¼ teaspoon pepper
1 tablespoon lemon juice
½ teaspoon grated lemon peel
1 clove garlic, minced
2 tablespoons salad oil
2 eggs, beaten
1 can (13 ounces) evaporated milk

1. In a 10-inch glass skillet, combine rice, green pepper, parsley, cheese, onion, salt, and pepper; blend well. Stir in lemon juice, lemon peel, garlic, oil, eggs, and milk.
2. Cook 10 to 12 minutes, rotating dish one-quarter turn halfway through cooking time.
3. Rest 5 minutes before serving.

6 to 8 servings

Conventional oven: Bake at 350°F 45 minutes.

Spanish Rice

1 tablespoon butter
1½ cups chopped celery
1 cup chopped green pepper
1 cup chopped onion
½ to 1 tablespoon garlic salt
½ teaspoon cumin
½ teaspoon oregano
1 to 2 tablespoons chili powder
¾ cup dairy sour cream
3 cups cooked rice (page 24)
2 or 3 tomatoes, cut in wedges

1. In a 2-quart glass casserole, combine butter, celery, green pepper, and onion. Cook 5 to 7 minutes, stirring halfway through cooking time.
2. Blend garlic salt, cumin, oregano, and chili powder into sour cream and add with rice to vegetable mixture. Arrange tomato wedges on top.
3. Cook, covered, 2 to 3 minutes. Remove cover, rotate dish one-quarter turn, and cook 2 to 3 minutes more.
4. Rest, covered, 5 minutes before serving.

5 or 6 servings

Oatmeal

1½ cups uncooked old-fashioned oats
3 cups water
¾ teaspoon salt

1. In a 2-quart glass casserole, combine oats, water, and salt. Stir to blend.
2. Cook 7 to 9 minutes, stirring halfway through cooking time.
3. Cover and rest 5 minutes before serving.

4 to 6 servings

Microwave Granola

8 cups uncooked oats, quick or old-fashioned
1½ cups shredded coconut
¾ cup wheat germ
½ cup pinenuts, sunflower seeds, or walnuts, chopped
¼ cup sesame seed
½ cup brown sugar
½ cup honey
½ cup salad oil

1. In a large glass mixing bowl, combine oats, coconut, wheat germ, nuts, sesame seed, brown sugar, honey, and oil. Stir until well mixed.
2. Cook 15 to 18 minutes, stirring every 5 minutes to mix well.
3. Rest until cool. Store in tightly covered container and use as needed for cereal and toppings for cakes, cookies, and puddings.

About 10 cups

CHEESE AND EGGS

Cheese and eggs both need careful handling when cooked in the microwave oven. Cheese often requires only melting, so it should be added near the end of the cooking time; avoid overcooking, or the cheese may become stringy and tough. Grated or shredded cheese is better for microwave cooking than chunks, and process cheese usually blends more easily with other foods.

Eggs can be very temperamental when cooked in the microwave. Most people don't believe that an egg will cook in 25 to 35 seconds, but it will! Never try to cook an egg in its shell—the internal pressure will cause it to explode. Eggs should be removed from the shell and cooked in a glass dish or individual container. The egg yolk has a very high fat content which is very suitable for the doughnut effect which occurs with microwave cooking. By covering the dish with plastic wrap during the cooking time, the egg will hold in the heat to finish cooking the white without overcooking the yolk.

Eggs scrambled in the microwave need less attention than in conventional cooking. They can be covered for a softer texture, or left uncovered for a drier dish. For a main dish, vegetables and cheese can be added after the eggs are cooked.

Cottage Cheese Meatless Loaf

1 cup chopped walnuts
1 medium onion, finely chopped
1 cup corn or whole wheat flakes, crushed
1 cup finely chopped celery leaves
1 pint small curd creamed cottage cheese
2 eggs
½ teaspoon sage
¼ cup salad oil
½ teaspoon salt
1 to 2 teaspoons soy sauce

1. In a large mixing bowl, combine walnuts, onion, cereal, celery leaves, cottage cheese, eggs, sage, oil, salt, and soy sauce; mix well.
2. Pack mixture lightly in a 2-quart glass casserole, making a well in the center and placing an empty glass, open end up, in the center of the dish.
3. Cook 14 to 16 minutes, rotating dish one-quarter turn halfway through cooking time.
4. Rest 10 minutes before serving.

5 or 6 servings

Note: This loaf has even more flavor when made the day before and reheated before serving.

Cheese Fondue

½ pound Swiss cheese, shredded
2 tablespoons flour
½ teaspoon salt
¼ teaspoon garlic powder
¼ teaspoon nutmeg
¼ teaspoon white pepper
½ cup milk
2 tablespoons kirsch (optional)
French bread, cut in 1-inch cubes

1. In a 2-quart glass casserole, mix together the cheese, flour, salt, garlic powder, nutmeg, and white pepper. Add milk and, if desired, kirsch; stir to mix.
2. Cook, covered, 3 to 4 minutes, stirring once or twice. Rest covered, 5 minutes.
3. Spear cubes of bread and dip in fondue. If fondue cools, reheat 1 to 2 minutes.

3 or 4 servings

Welsh Rabbit

2 tablespoons butter
2 cups shredded Cheddar cheese
1 cup beer
½ teaspoon dry mustard
¼ teaspoon Tabasco
4 toasted hamburger buns

1. In a 2-quart glass casserole, heat butter 30 seconds. Add cheese and cook 1 to 2 minutes until cheese begins to melt, stirring halfway through cooking time.
2. Stir in beer, mustard, and Tabasco. Heat 1 minute.
3. Serve hot on toasted buns.

4 sandwiches

Quick Cheese Fondue

1 can (10½ ounces) condensed
    Cheddar cheese soup
⅓ cup milk
¼ teaspoon garlic powder
¼ teaspoon nutmeg
1½ cups shredded Swiss cheese

1. In a 4-cup glass measure, blend soup and milk; cook 3 to 4 minutes, stirring halfway through cooking time.
2. Add garlic powder and nutmeg; stir to blend. Blend in cheese.
3. Cook 2 to 3 minutes, stirring every minute, until cheese is melted.
4. Serve immediately while warm.

2 cups fondue

Scrambled Eggs

2 tablespoons butter
4 eggs
¼ cup milk or water
¼ teaspoon salt

1. In a deep 1-quart glass dish, heat butter 30 seconds. Add eggs, milk, and salt; stir to blend.
2. Cook, covered, 2½ to 4 minutes, stirring halfway through cooking time. Stir to scramble. For firmer eggs, cook longer length of time recommended.
3. Rest, covered, 5 minutes before serving.

2 or 3 servings

Omelet: Follow recipe for Scrambled Eggs. Place egg mixture in a 9-inch glass pie plate. Cook 2½ to 4 minutes, stirring halfway through cooking time. Omit stirring at the end of cooking time. Fold in half and slide onto a plate.

2 or 3 servings

Fried Egg

Egg

1. Break egg into 10-ounce custard cup. Pierce yolk with a fork and cover with plastic wrap.
2. Cook as follows, rotating one-quarter turn halfway through cooking time: 1 egg, 25 to 35 seconds; 2 eggs, 1 minute to 1¼ minutes; 3 eggs, 1½ to 1¾ minutes; 4 eggs, 2 to 2¼ minutes. If a soft yolk is preferred, cook the shorter time. If a firmer yolk is desired, cook the longer time.
3. Rest, covered, 5 minutes before serving, if desired.

Note: If cupcaker is used, place a small amount of butter in the bottom of paper baking cup in each well. Break egg into each cup and cover with plastic wrap. Cook as directed for fried eggs in custard cup, but reduce cooking time 5 to 10 seconds for each egg.

Note: Never cook an egg in its shell in the microwave oven. Steam forms readily, and the egg might explode the shell.

Poached Egg

Egg
Water

1. Place ½ cup water in a 10-ounce custard cup and heat 30 seconds.
2. Break egg into hot water and cover with plastic wrap.
3. Cook, following times indicated for Fried Egg (above).
4. Rest, covered, 5 minutes before serving.

Bacon and Egg Turbans

6 slices bacon
6 eggs
2 tablespoons dairy sour cream

1. Arrange bacon on roasting rack in a 2-quart glass baking dish and cook as follows: 1 slice for 1 minute; 2 slices for 1½ minutes; 3 slices for 2½ minutes; 4 slices for 3 minutes; and 6 slices for 4 minutes. Limp, not crisp, bacon is desired.
2. Arrange a bacon slice in a circle in the bottom of a 6-ounce glass custard cup. Break egg in cup over bacon. Pierce yolk with fork, and top egg with 1 teaspoon sour cream.
3. Place cups in a circle on a 9-inch glass pie plate. Add 1 cup water to glass plate and cover with plastic wrap. Cook until done, as follows, rotating plate one-quarter turn halfway through cooking time: 1 egg, 1½ to 2 minutes; 2 eggs, 2 to 3 minutes; 3 eggs, 2½ to 3½ minutes; 4 eggs, 3 to 4 minutes; 6 eggs, 4 to 5 minutes.
4. Rest, covered, 1 minute after cooking. Invert custard cup on **buttered toasted English muffin** and serve immediately.

6 servings

Marvelous Eggs

3 tablespoons butter
1 tablespoon minced green onion
6 eggs, slightly beaten
⅓ cup milk
½ teaspoon salt
¼ teaspoon lemon juice
1 package (3 ounces) cream cheese,
    cut in ½-inch cubes

1. In a 2-quart glass casserole, heat butter 30 seconds. Add onion and cook 2 minutes, stirring once. Stir in eggs, milk, salt, and lemon juice.
2. Cook, covered, 4 to 5 minutes, stirring every 2 minutes. When almost set, lightly fold in cream cheese.
3. Cook 1 minute longer, rest 5 minutes, and serve.

4 servings

Mushroom Eggs on Toast

1 pound fresh mushrooms, cleaned
    and sliced
¼ cup butter
4 slices hot buttered toast
2 tablespoons butter
2 tablespoons flour
1 cup milk
½ cup grated Parmesan cheese
¼ teaspoon dry mustard
4 poached eggs (page 29)
    Paprika (optional)

1. In a 1-quart glass casserole, cook mushrooms in ¼ cup butter 3 to 4 minutes, stirring halfway through cooking time. Cover each slice toast with one-fourth of the mushrooms.
2. In a 2-cup glass measure, heat 2 tablespoons butter 30 seconds. Stir in flour to blend. Stir in milk and cook 2 to 3 minutes, stirring every minute, until sauce becomes thick. Add cheese and dry mustard; stir to blend.
3. Place an egg on top of mushrooms on each toast slice and cover with sauce. Sprinkle with paprika, if desired.

3 or 4 servings

Confetti Eggs

2 tablespoons butter
½ cup diced ham
2 green onions, including tops,
    chopped
4 eggs
    Dash Tabasco
½ teaspoon salt
¼ teaspoon pepper

1. In a 2-quart glass casserole, cook butter, ham, and green onions 3 to 4 minutes, stirring every minute.
2. Add eggs, Tabasco, salt, and pepper; stir to blend.
3. Cook, covered, 3 to 4 minutes, stirring halfway through cooking time.
4. Rest, covered, 5 minutes.

3 or 4 servings

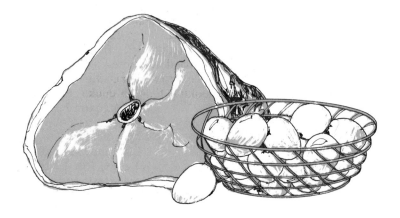

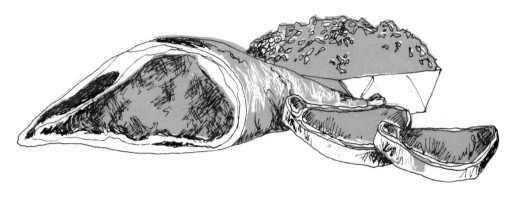

MEAT

Tender cuts of meat generally cook better than less tender cuts. For steaks, chops, and other foods that you prefer grilled or seared, do this prior to cooking on the conventional range or in the microwave ceramic browner. It is best to select those cuts of meat that are more evenly shaped. Sometimes this is not possible. If not, they must be arranged on the cooking dish so that the thicker or denser parts are placed near the outside of the dish and the smaller portions near the center where there is less energy.

We prefer to place all meat that is to be roasted on a roasting rack. This allows drippings to collect in the bottom of the dish, without the meat sitting in them. If a large amount accumulates, it should be removed periodically during the cooking time.

Unevenly shaped pieces of meat should be shielded prior to cooking. The shielding will not prevent cooking in these areas because they will cook by transfer of heat from the cooked portion to the shielded portion.

To determine the cooking time for meats allow:

6–7 minutes per pound for rare
7–8 minutes per pound for medium
8–9 minutes per pound for well done

Meats should be rotated one quarter or one half turn halfway through the cooking time to cook evenly. When cooking a roast, it should also be turned over one quarter turn halfway through the cooking time. If the roast won't sit evenly after turning, prop it up with a glass cup or dish. Allow the roast to rest 15 minutes after cooking before serving. It will finish cooking during this time. If you prefer additional crisping and browning of the surface, place it under a hot broiler element for a few minutes. Generally this won't be necessary, because the meat browns nicely in the microwave.

Be careful to avoid overcooking the meat, or it will be dry and tough. More time can be added after the carry-over cooking time if necessary.

HAM: Canned, precooked hams do not need cooking. They can be heated 5 or 6 minutes per pound to reach the serving temperature.

PORK: All cuts of pork cook very well in the microwave because of the high fat content. Roasts may be cooked like other roasts but should be cooked until well done—8 or 9 minutes per pound. Barbecue sauces and gravy may be added to smaller cuts to produce a good brown color.

The cooking time for bacon depends on the thickness, sugar, salt, and fat content and will vary from one package to another. A homemaker who buys the same brand consistently will find the cooking time she prefers for the crispness desired.

Beef Roast

5- to 6-pound beef roast (rib, rump, or chuck)

1. Place roast on roasting rack in a 2-quart glass baking dish. Shield protruding corners or bone ends with foil. Do not allow foil to touch inside walls of oven.
2. Cook, using the following times: for rare meat, 6 to 7 minutes per pound; for medium, 7 to 8 minutes per pound; and for well-done, 8 to 9 minutes per pound. Turn roast over and rotate the dish one-quarter turn halfway through cooking time.
3. Rest 10 to 15 minutes before carving and serving.

10 to 12 servings

Chinese Tomato Beef

2 pounds beef steak (sirloin, round, flank, or chuck)
2 tablespoons sugar
½ cup soy sauce
1 clove garlic, minced
¼ teaspoon ginger
3 tablespoons salad oil
2 large green peppers, cut in strips
3 green onions, cut in 1-inch pieces
2 large tomatoes, peeled and cut in wedges
2 tablespoons cornstarch
¼ cup water

1. Slice steak diagonally across the grain in ⅛-inch-thick slices. Meat will slice easier if placed in the freezer 30 minutes.
2. In a 2-cup glass measure, combine sugar, soy sauce, garlic, and ginger. Pour over meat in a 9-inch baking dish. Marinate at least 30 minutes, turning meat occasionally.
3. Preheat browning dish 6 minutes. Remove meat from marinade; reserve marinade. Add oil and meat to dish. Fry meat 5 to 6 minutes in microwave oven, stirring halfway through cooking time. Drain cooking juices into marinade.
4. Stir green pepper and onion into meat. Cook 3 to 4 minutes, stirring halfway through cooking time. Top with tomato wedges.
5. In a 1-cup glass measure, combine cornstarch and water, and blend with marinade. Cook 1 to 2 minutes, stirring halfway through cooking time, until thickened. Pour over meat and vegetables and heat 1 to 2 minutes.
6. Rest 5 minutes and serve over **hot fluffy rice.**

8 servings

Marinated Flank Steak

⅓ cup soy sauce
2 tablespoons vinegar
¼ cup minced onion
¼ teaspoon garlic powder
1½ teaspoons ground ginger
2 tablespoons sugar
2 pounds beef flank steak

1. In a 2-quart glass baking dish, blend soy sauce, vinegar, onion, garlic powder, ginger, and sugar. Dip meat in mixture and marinate 4 hours, turning occasionally.
2. Cut steak into serving pieces. Pound to tenderize.
3. Return to 2-quart dish with sauce and cook, covered, 12 to 14 minutes, rotating dish one-quarter turn halfway through cooking time.
4. Serve with **hot rice.**

6 or 7 servings

Tomato-Leek Soup, 16;
Frankfurter Reuben, 23

Swiss Steak

1½ to 2 pounds beef round steak, cut in serving pieces and floured
2 tablespoons salad oil
1 can (10 ounces) condensed cream of mushroom soup
1 soup can water
½ teaspoon salt
Dash pepper
¼ teaspoon garlic powder
1 small onion, chopped
½ cup chopped green pepper

1. Brown meat in hot oil on range in a conventional skillet or in microwave oven. To brown in microwave oven, preheat browning skillet 6 minutes. Pour oil in hot pan and cook meat 1½ minutes, turn over, and cook for 1 minute. Place meat in a 2-quart glass casserole.
2. In a mixing bowl, blend soup with water, salt, pepper, and garlic powder. Pour over meat. Arrange onion and green pepper on top.
3. Cook, covered, 10 minutes; rest 5 minutes. Rotate dish one-quarter turn and cook 7 to 8 minutes; rest 5 minutes. Rotate dish one-quarter turn and cook 10 minutes.
4. Rest 10 minutes before serving.

6 to 8 servings

Sukiyaki

1 pound beef sirloin steak, diagonally sliced in very thin long strips
2 cups celery, diagonally sliced in ½-inch pieces
2 medium onions, cut in wedges
1 bunch green onions, including tops, cut in 1-inch lengths
2 cups sliced fresh mushrooms
2 cans (5 ounces each) bamboo shoots, drained
½ cup soy sauce
¼ cup sugar
½ cup saké or beef stock

1. Stir-fry meat in conventional skillet on top of range, or using microwave oven, preheat browning dish 6 minutes, add meat, and fry 2 to 3 minutes until well browned.
2. In a 2-quart glass casserole, combine celery, onion, green onion, mushrooms, and bamboo shoots with meat. Cook, covered, 6 to 8 minutes, stirring halfway through cooking time. Rest, covered, 10 minutes.
3. In a 1-cup glass measure, blend soy sauce, sugar, and saké. Cook 1 minute, stirring halfway through cooking time.
4. Pour sauce over vegetables and stir to blend.
5. Serve hot over **fluffy rice**.

4 to 6 servings

Teriyaki Steak

2 to 2½ pounds beef chuck or sirloin steak
¾ teaspoon ginger
2 tablespoons sugar
¼ cup salad oil
¼ cup soy sauce
2 tablespoons sherry
1 clove garlic, minced

1. Slice meat diagonally into ⅛-inch-thick strips. Meat will slice easier if placed in the freezer 30 minutes.
2. In a 2-cup glass measure, combine ginger, sugar, oil, soy sauce, sherry, and garlic. Stir to blend. Pour over meat strips and marinate from 1 hour to overnight.
3. Preheat browning dish 5 minutes. Reserving marinade, remove meat from marinade and add to hot dish; fry 2 to 3 minutes, stirring after every minute. (See Note.)
4. Pour marinade over meat and cook 4 to 5 minutes more, stirring after every minute.
5. Serve hot over **fluffy rice**.

4 to 6 servings

Note: If desired, meat may be browned in a conventional skillet on top of the range, and then transferred to a 2-quart glass baking dish.

Chinese Tomato Beef, 32

Favorite Meat Loaf

1¾ pounds ground beef
¾ cup uncooked oats
¼ cup finely minced onion
¼ cup chopped celery
1½ teaspoons salt
½ teaspoon pepper
1 cup tomato juice
2 eggs
½ cup ketchup

1. In a large mixing bowl, combine ground beef, oats, onion, celery, salt, pepper, tomato juice, and eggs, blending evenly.
2. Turn mixture into a 9-inch glass pie plate with a glass, open end up, in center of dish, packing lightly.
3. Cook 6 to 8 minutes, rotating dish one-quarter turn halfway through cooking time.
4. Remove excess drippings. Pour ketchup over top, cover with waxed paper, and cook 6 to 8 minutes, rotating dish one-quarter turn halfway through cooking time.
5. Rest, covered, 10 minutes before serving.

4 to 6 servings

Rice-Stuffed Hamburger

1 pound ground beef
½ teaspoon salt
2 tablespoons chopped onion
1 can (8 ounces) tomato sauce
2 cups cooked rice
4 slices mozzarella cheese

1. In a mixing bowl, combine ground beef, salt, onion, and tomato sauce.
2. Spread half of mixture evenly over bottom of an 8-inch square glass dish. Lightly press rice onto meat. Layer cheese over rice. Spread remaining meat mixture on top.
3. Cook 6 to 8 minutes, rotating dish one-quarter turn halfway through cooking time. Spoon off drippings.
4. Rest 10 minutes before slicing.

4 to 6 servings

Conventional oven: Bake at 375°F 30 to 40 minutes.

Cheese Meat Loaf

2 slices bread
⅓ cup milk
½ medium onion, chopped
2 eggs
1 pound ground beef
½ cup shredded Cheddar cheese
1 teaspoon salt
¼ cup tomato sauce

1. Soak bread in milk.
2. In a large mixing bowl, combine bread, milk, onion, eggs, beef, cheese, and salt. Shape into loaf and place in glass loaf dish.
3. Cook 6 to 8 minutes, rotating dish one-quarter turn halfway through cooking time.
4. Pour tomato sauce over top and heat 1 minute.
5. Rest 10 minutes before slicing.

About 4 servings

Conventional oven: Bake at 375°F 1 hour.

Note: Loaf may be shaped in a ring for more even cooking.

German Meatball Stew

1½ pounds ground beef
1 egg
1½ teaspoons salt
½ teaspoon pepper
1 large potato, pared and grated
½ teaspoon ginger
2 large onions, sliced
2 tablespoons salad oil

1. In a large mixing bowl, combine ground beef, egg, salt, pepper, potato, and ginger, blending evenly. Shape 24 meatballs.
2. Arrange meatballs evenly in a 2-quart glass baking dish. Cook 10 to 12 minutes, stirring halfway through cooking time.
3. In a 3-quart glass casserole, combine onions and oil and cook 2 minutes. Stir in carrots and cook, covered, 5 to 6 minutes.

1 **pound carrots, pared and sliced**
1½ **cups beer or beef broth**
1½ **cups water**
¼ **cup flour**
   Fluffy Dumplings (optional)

4. Add meatballs, beer, and 1 cup water to casserole. Bring to boiling and cook 10 to 12 minutes, rotating one-quarter turn halfway through cooking time.
5. In a 2-cup glass measure, combine ½ cup water with flour and stir to blend. Stir flour mixture into liquid in stew. If desired, drop dumpling dough on stew. Cook, covered, 7 to 10 minutes, rotating one-quarter turn halfway through cooking time.
6. Rest, covered, 10 minutes before serving.

6 to 8 servings

Fluffy Dumplings: In a small mixing bowl, combine **1½ cups all-purpose flour, 1 tablespoon baking powder, ½ teaspoon salt,** and **¼ cup chopped parsley.** Stir in **⅔ cup milk** until ingredients are moistened. Bring **2½ cups stock** to boiling. Drop dough by rounded teaspoonfuls onto boiling stock. Cook, covered, 7 to 10 minutes, rotating dish one-quarter turn halfway through cooking time. Rest 5 minutes before serving.

Many-Way Meatballs

1 **pound ground beef**
¼ **cup dry bread crumbs**
¼ **cup minced onion**
1 **egg**
¼ **teaspoon salt**
1 **can (10½ ounces) condensed**
   Cheddar cheese, cream of celery,
   or cream of mushroom soup
½ **cup water**
2 **tablespoons parsley flakes**

1. In a mixing bowl, combine beef, bread crumbs, onion, egg, and salt. Shape into 16 meatballs, and place in a 2-quart baking dish.
2. Cook, covered, 5 to 6 minutes, stirring halfway through cooking time. Pour off drippings.
3. Stir in soup, water, and parsley. Cover and cook 6 to 8 minutes, stirring halfway through cooking time.
4. Rest 5 minutes before serving.

3 or 4 servings

Sweet-and-Sour Meatballs

1 **pound ground beef**
1 **egg**
1 **tablespoon cornstarch**
2 **tablespoons finely minced green**
   onion
1 **teaspoon salt**
   Dash pepper
1 **can (16 ounces) pineapple chunks,**
   drained (reserve juice)
½ **cup sugar**
3 **tablespoons cornstarch**
1 **tablespoon soy sauce**
3 **tablespoons vinegar**
4 **cups cooked rice**

1. In a medium mixing bowl, blend ground beef, egg, cornstarch, onion, salt, and pepper. Shape 1 tablespoon mixture around each pineapple chunk. Reserve remaining pineapple.
2. In a glass pie plate, arrange meatballs evenly around edge. Cook 5 to 7 minutes, stirring to rearrange meatballs halfway through cooking time.
3. In a 2-cup glass measure, blend sugar, cornstarch, soy sauce, vinegar, and reserved pineapple juice.
4. Cook sauce 2 to 3 minutes, or until mixture begins to boil, stirring after every minute.
5. Pour sauce and remaining pineapple chunks over meatballs, mixing gently.
6. Serve over cooked rice.

4 servings

Lamb Roast

5- to 6-pound lamb leg roast

1. Place roast, fat side down, on roasting rack in a 2-quart glass baking dish. Shield protruding corners or bones with foil. Do not allow foil to touch walls inside microwave oven.
2. Cook, using the following times: for medium, 7 to 8 minutes per pound; and for well-done, 8 to 9 minutes per pound. Turn roast over and rotate the dish one-quarter turn halfway through cooking time.
3. Rest 15 minutes before carving and serving.

8 to 10 servings

Glazed Ham Steak

½ **cup buttermilk**
1 **smoked ham center slice, about 1 inch thick, cut in serving pieces**
1 **teaspoon dry mustard**
1 **teaspoon flour**
¼ **teaspoon pepper**
2 **egg yolks**
1 **cup buttermilk**
  Paprika

1. Generously brush ½ cup buttermilk on both sides of ham slice. Arrange on roasting rack in a 2-quart glass baking dish.
2. Cook 7 to 8 minutes, rotating dish one-quarter turn halfway through cooking time.
3. In a 2-cup glass measure, combine mustard, flour, pepper, and egg yolks, blending well. Slowly add 1 cup buttermilk, stirring until combined.
4. Cook 2 to 3 minutes, stirring every 30 seconds, until mixture thickens.
5. Spoon over individual ham portions, arranged in serving dish. Sprinkle with paprika. Reheat 1 to 2 minutes if needed.

6 to 8 servings

Apple-Stuffed Pork Chops

1 **cup bread crumbs**
1 **cup pared and cubed cooking apples**
2 **tablespoons butter**
1 **teaspoon salt**
4 **to 6 medium pork chops**

1. In a small mixing bowl, combine bread crumbs, apples, butter, and salt. Cook 2 to 3 minutes, stirring after every minute.
2. Cut a slit in each pork chop and stuff with bread-crumb mixture. Arrange in a 2-quart glass baking dish.
3. Cook, covered, 16 to 20 minutes, rotating dish one-quarter turn halfway through cooking time.
4. Rest, covered, 10 minutes before serving.

4 to 6 servings

Tangy Pork Chops

4 **to 6 pork chops**
  Prepared mustard
1 **can (10½ ounces) condensed cream of celery soup**

1. Spread both sides of each pork chop with mustard and place in a 10-inch glass baking dish.
2. Cook pork chops 6 to 8 minutes, rotating dish one-quarter turn halfway through cooking time.
3. Remove drippings from pan. Pour soup over pork chops. Cook, covered, 5 to 6 minutes, rotating dish one-quarter turn halfway through cooking time.
4. Rest, covered, 5 minutes before serving.

4 to 6 servings

Barbecued Meatballs

1 pound ground beef
1 egg
1 teaspoon anise seed
1 teaspoon salt
¼ teaspoon pepper
1 bottle (14 ounces) ketchup
¼ cup chopped onion
¼ cup vinegar
½ cup brown sugar
¼ cup salad oil
¼ cup water
2 teaspoons Worcestershire sauce
½ teaspoon Tabasco
1 clove garlic, minced
1 teaspoon salt

1. In a medium mixing bowl, blend ground beef, egg, anise, 1 teaspoon salt, and pepper. Shape into 24 meatballs.
2. Arrange meatballs evenly toward outer edges of a 2-quart glass baking dish. Cook 5 to 6 minutes, rearranging meatballs in dish halfway through cooking time. Drain off juices.
3. In a 2-quart glass baking dish, combine ketchup, onion, vinegar, brown sugar, oil, water, Worcestershire sauce, Tabasco, garlic, and 1 teaspoon salt. Cook sauce 4 minutes, stirring halfway through cooking time.
4. Add meatballs to sauce and cook 4 to 5 minutes, stirring halfway through cooking time.
5. Serve over **cooked rice** or **noodles.**

4 to 6 servings

Spareribs

1½ to 2 pounds lean spareribs
½ cup water
2 cups Barbecue Sauce (page 18)

1. In a covered 2-quart glass casserole, arrange spareribs in serving-size pieces toward edges of dish. Add ¼ cup water, cover, and cook 6 minutes, rotating dish one-quarter turn halfway through cooking time. Pour off water and drippings.
2. Add another ¼ cup water, cover, and cook again 6 minutes, rotating dish one-quarter turn halfway through cooking time. Pour off drippings.
3. Arrange spareribs in a 10-inch glass serving dish and cover with Barbecue Sauce.
4. Cook, uncovered, 4 to 5 minutes, rotating dish one-quarter turn halfway through cooking time.
5. Rest, uncovered, 5 minutes before serving.

4 servings

Fresh Ham

5- to 6-pound cook-before-eating ham

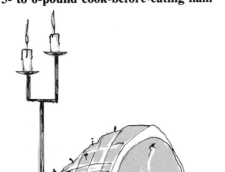

1. Place ham on roasting rack in a 2-quart glass baking dish. Shield protruding corners or shank end with foil. Do not allow foil to touch walls inside microwave oven.
2. Cook 40 to 50 minutes, allowing 8 to 9 minutes per pound. Turn ham over and rotate dish one-quarter turn halfway through cooking time.
3. Rest 10 to 15 minutes before carving or serving.

10 to 12 servings

Cooked Ham: Follow recipe for Fresh Ham, but allow 6 to 7 minutes per pound cooking time, or 30 to 40 minutes for a 5- to 6-pound ham.

Fresh Pork Roast: Follow recipe for Fresh Ham, allowing 8 to 9 minutes per pound cooking time.

Breakfast Kabobs

8 ounces link pork sausage
6 ounces Canadian bacon, or 12
    ounces canned luncheon meat
1 can (8 ounces) pineapple chunks,
    drained
16 maraschino cherries
    Maple syrup
8 bamboo skewers

1. Cut each sausage link in 3 or 4 pieces. Cut bacon in small cubes.
2. Thread meat and fruit alternately on skewers. Arrange in a 2-quart glass baking dish and brush with maple syrup.
3. Cook, covered, 4 to 6 minutes, rotating one-quarter turn and basting with syrup halfway through cooking time.

4 to 6 servings

Sausage Ring

1 pound bulk pork sausage
2 eggs
2 tablespoons minced onion
½ cup bread crumbs
2 tablespoons parsley flakes

1. In a 1-quart glass casserole, blend sausage, eggs, onion, bread crumbs, and parsley flakes. Mold into a ring and place a small glass, open end up, in the center of the ring.
2. Cook 5 to 6 minutes, rotating dish one-quarter turn halfway through cooking time.
3. Rest 5 minutes, remove glass from center, and invert ring on plate to serve. Center may be filled with **cooked rice** or **noodles.** If using for breakfast, center may be filled with **scrambled eggs.**

4 or 5 servings

Note: Leftover Sausage Ring makes good sandwiches when reheated.

Bacon

Cooking time for bacon will vary depending on the quality and curing process of the bacon, the thickness of the bacon slices, and if it has been standing at room temperature for any length of time.

Slices bacon

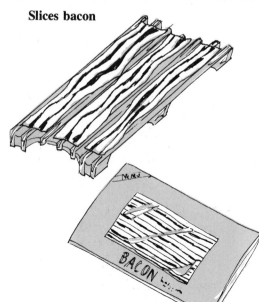

1. Arrange bacon on roasting rack or on crumpled paper towels in a 2-quart glass baking dish. Heat bacon 30 seconds to make separating slices easy. If there is more than 1 layer of bacon, place crumpled paper towel between layers. Cover with paper towel to prevent spattering.
2. Cook until desired crispness is reached, using the following timing guides: cook 1 slice bacon 1 to 1½ minutes; 2 slices, 2 to 2½ minutes; 4 slices, 4 to 4½ minutes; 6 slices, 5½ to 6 minutes; and 8 slices, 6 to 7 minutes. Rotate dish one-quarter turn halfway through cooking time.
3. To cook 1 pound of bacon, place separated slices in a glass baking dish. Heat about 4 minutes; rearrange bacon slices so cooked slices are in the center and uncooked pieces are near the edges. Continue cooking 4 to 5 minutes, or until done.

POULTRY

The microwave gives good results with many dishes using poultry. If a recipe calls for cooked chicken or turkey, this can be easily cooked and added to the recipe later. Chicken breasts cook very nicely in the microwave. Fried chicken is also very good cooked in the microwave. Frying chickens should be selected because stewing chickens will become tough during the short cooking time needed in the microwave. Arrange with thighs, legs, and breasts near the outside, and wings, back, etc. near the center. Turn pieces over halfway through cooking time.

It is important to arrange the poultry properly at the start of the cooking time. If you are cooking whole birds, shield wings and leg ends at the start of the cooking time. Whole birds should be turned over halfway through the cooking time. We prefer to start the cooking with the breast down and finish with the breast up.

Microwave Fried Chicken

1 **broiler-fryer (2½ to 3 pounds)**
1 **cup corn flake crumbs**
¼ **cup butter**
  Paprika

1. Wash chicken and coat with crumbs. In a 1-cup glass measure, heat butter 45 seconds.
2. On roasting rack in a 2-quart glass baking dish, arrange chicken with meatier pieces around edges of dish, and smaller pieces, such as wings, in the center. Pour a small amount of butter over each piece. Sprinkle with paprika.
3. Cook 10 to 12 minutes. Turn chicken pieces over and coat each piece with remaining butter and paprika. Cook 10 to 12 minutes.
4. Rest 5 minutes before serving.

4 to 6 servings

Note: The chicken may be covered during cooking, which will steam the chicken, producing a soft, not crisp, skin. If the chicken is in a glass ceramic baking dish or is transferred to a metal pan, additional browning can be achieved by placing cooked chicken under a conventional broiler 1 to 2 minutes.

Creamed Chicken Casserole

4 chicken breasts, halved
1 can (10½ ounces) condensed cream
    of chicken soup
2 tablespoons brandy
½ cup dairy sour cream
2 green onions, chopped
    Dash pepper
¼ cup cashews
    Parsley, chopped
    Paprika

1. Wash chicken and pat dry. Arrange in a 2-quart baking dish. Cook 10 to 12 minutes, rotating one-quarter turn halfway through cooking time.
2. In a mixing bowl blend soup, brandy, sour cream, onion, pepper, and cashews. Pour over chicken.
3. Cook, covered, 12 to 15 minutes, rotating one-quarter turn halfway through cooking time.
4. Garnish with parsley or paprika, if desired.

4 servings

Chicken Hawaiian

1½ cups sliced celery
1 green pepper, cut in strips
3 tablespoons butter
3 cups cubed cooked chicken
1 can (21 ounces) pineapple pie
    filling
¼ cup soy sauce
2 teaspoons instant chicken bouillon
    Chow mein noodles
    Parsley (optional)

1. In a 2-quart glass casserole, blend celery, green pepper, and butter. Cook 3 to 4 minutes, stirring halfway through cooking time.
2. Add chicken, pie filling, soy sauce, and bouillon; mix well.
3. Cook, covered, 10 to 12 minutes, stirring halfway through cooking time.
4. Serve over chow mein noodles and garnish with parsley, if desired.

5 or 6 servings

Dinner Chicken Wings

2 to 3 pounds chicken wings
1 teaspoon ginger
1 teaspoon dry mustard
1 tablespoon brown sugar
⅓ cup soy sauce
3 tablespoons salad oil
3 cloves garlic, quartered
2 tablespoons sesame seed

1. Clip wing tips from each wing. Divide each wing at the joint, in two pieces. Place wing pieces in a 2-quart glass baking dish.
2. In a mixing bowl, blend ginger, mustard, brown sugar, soy sauce, oil, and garlic. Pour over chicken pieces and marinate overnight.
3. Remove the garlic pieces from the marinade. Cook the chicken in marinade 12 to 14 minutes, rotating dish one-quarter turn halfway through cooking time.
4. Rest, covered with waxed paper, 10 minutes. Pour off marinade. Sprinkle chicken with sesame seed and heat 1 minute.

5 or 6 servings

Note: Dinner Chicken Wings may be served with rice for a main dish or used as an appetizer.

Chicken and Broccoli

2 packages (10 ounces each) frozen
    broccoli
3 chicken breasts, cooked and cut in
    serving pieces
1 can (10½ ounces) condensed cream
    of chicken soup
⅔ cup mayonnaise
½ cup milk
½ cup shredded Cheddar cheese
1 can (6 ounces) water chestnuts,
    drained and sliced
1 teaspoon lemon juice
½ teaspoon curry powder
½ cup chopped cashews
½ cup bread crumbs

1. Pierce broccoli packages and cook 6 to 8 minutes, rotating packages one-quarter turn halfway through cooking time.
2. Arrange broccoli evenly in bottom of a 2-quart baking dish and layer chicken on top.
3. In a small mixing bowl, blend soup, mayonnaise, milk, cheese, water chestnuts, lemon juice, curry powder, and cashews. Pour over chicken and broccoli. Sprinkle bread crumbs on top.
4. Cook 10 to 12 minutes, rotating dish one-quarter turn halfway through cooking time.
5. Rest, covered, 10 minutes before serving.

4 to 6 servings

Chicken Enchiladas

1 onion, finely chopped
2 tablespoons butter
4 cups chopped cooked chicken or
    turkey
1 can (4 ounces) chopped green
    chilies
1 can (10½ ounces) condensed
    cream of chicken soup
12 frozen corn tortillas
1 can (10½ ounces) condensed
    cream of celery soup
1½ cups dairy sour cream
1 pound Cheddar or Monterey Jack
    cheese, shredded

1. In a large glass mixing bowl, cook onion in butter 2 minutes, stirring halfway through cooking time. Blend in chicken, chilies, and cream of chicken soup.
2. Defrost tortillas until soft and easy to roll, about 1 minute. Spread about 3 tablespoons chicken mixture on each tortilla, roll, and secure with a wooden pick. Arrange in two 9-inch glass baking dishes.
3. In a small mixing bowl, blend cream of celery soup and sour cream. Pour over enchiladas.
4. Cook each dish 10 to 12 minutes, rotating one-quarter turn halfway through cooking time.
5. Sprinkle ½ pound of the cheese over top of each dish and heat for 1 minute.
6. Rest, covered, 10 minutes. Remove wooden picks and serve.

6 to 8 servings

Note: The enchiladas may be prepared through step 3, and then frozen immediately. Continue with steps 4 and 5 when casserole has been thawed and is ready to heat.

Chicken and Rice Dinner

¾ cup packaged precooked rice
1 can (10½ ounces) condensed cream
    of mushroom soup
1 can (4 ounces) mushroom pieces
    (undrained)
¼ cup minced onion
1 can (13 ounces) evaporated milk
2 pounds chicken thighs and
    drumsticks

1. In a 3-quart glass casserole, blend rice, soup, mushrooms with liquid, onion, and milk. Cook, covered, 5 minutes, stirring halfway through cooking time.
2. Arrange chicken pieces in casserole. Cover, and cook 20 minutes, rotating dish one-quarter turn halfway through cooking time.
3. Rest, covered, 10 minutes before serving.

4 or 5 servings

Cranberry Chicken

1 broiler fryer (2½ to 3 pounds), cut in serving pieces
2 tablespoons lemon juice
3 tablespoons brown sugar
1 can (16 ounces) cranberry sauce

1. Arrange chicken pieces in a 2-quart glass baking dish with meatier pieces toward edge.
2. In a 1-cup glass measure, blend lemon juice, brown sugar, and cranberry sauce. Pour sauce evenly over chicken and cover dish with waxed paper.
3. Cook 20 minutes, basting with sauce and rotating dish one-quarter turn halfway through cooking time.
4. Rest, covered, 10 minutes before serving.

4 to 6 servings

Chicken Cacciatore

1 broiler fryer, cut up (2½ to 3 pounds)
¼ teaspoon salt
¼ teaspoon dry mustard
3 tablespoons salad oil
1 tablespoon vinegar
¼ teaspoon pepper
½ cup ketchup or chili sauce
1 tablespoon parsley flakes

1. In a 2-quart glass baking dish, arrange chicken pieces with meatier pieces toward the edge.
2. In a 2-cup measure, combine salt, dry mustard, oil, vinegar, pepper, ketchup, and parsley flakes; stir to blend. Pour sauce over chicken.
3. Cook, covered, 20 minutes, rotating dish one-quarter turn halfway through cooking time.
4. Rest, covered, 10 minutes before serving.

5 or 6 servings

Honey-Glazed Chicken

1 chicken (3 to 3½ pounds), cut in serving pieces
2 tablespoons butter
⅓ cup honey
1 teaspoon grated orange peel
1 teaspoon salt
¾ teaspoon garlic powder
1 teaspoon dry mustard
¼ teaspoon pepper

1. In a 2-quart glass baking dish, arrange chicken on a rack, if possible. Place meatier pieces in corners and small pieces in the center. Place giblets in the center tucked under back or wings. Cover with waxed paper.
2. Cook 15 minutes, rotating dish one-quarter turn halfway through cooking time.
3. In a 1-cup glass measure, heat butter 15 to 30 seconds. Add honey, orange peel, salt, garlic powder, dry mustard, and pepper; stir to blend. Heat mixture 30 seconds. Brush chicken pieces with honey-butter mixture.
4. Cook, uncovered, 4 minutes. Turn chicken pieces over and brush with remaining mixture. Return to oven and cook, uncovered, 3 to 4 minutes.
5. Remove chicken pieces to serving dish, pour drippings over chicken, and serve.

4 to 6 servings

Conventional oven: Bake at 375°F 1¼ hours.

Barbecued Cornish Hens

2 Cornish hens (1 pound each), cut in halves or left whole
½ cup Barbecue Sauce (page 18)

1. In an 8-inch square glass baking dish, arrange halves in corners. If hens are whole, place in diagonally opposite corners of dish. Brush with sauce. Cook, covered, 6 to 8 minutes.
2. Turn hens over, rotate dish one-quarter turn, and brush with remaining sauce. Cook, uncovered, 6 to 8 minutes.
3. Rest 5 minutes, and serve with **cooked rice.**

3 or 4 servings

Roast Turkey

8- to 15-pound turkey
2 tablespoons butter
1 tablespoon bottled brown bouquet
    sauce

1. Clean and prepare turkey for cooking as directed on turkey wrapper. Place turkey, breast down on roasting rack in a glass baking dish; cover with waxed paper.
2. Estimate the total cooking time. For an 8- to 12-pound turkey allow 7 to 8 minutes per pound, and for a 12- to 15-pound turkey allow 6 to 7 minutes per pound. Cook the turkey for a fourth of the estimated cooking time
3. Melt the butter in a custard cup and mix with the bottled brown bouquet sauce. Brush the turkey with the mixture. Cover the bottom half of wings and legs with small pieces of aluminum foil. Secure legs and wings close to body with string. Cover with waxed paper. Do not allow foil to touch inside walls of microwave oven.
4. Place turkey on its side and cook a fourth of estimated roasting time. Turn turkey on its other side and cook for another fourth of estimated roasting time. Cut strings to allow legs and wings to stand free, remove foil, place turkey breast up, and cook until turkey reaches internal temperature of 175°F. Each time turkey is turned rotate dish one-quarter turn and baste with drippings. Remove drippings as they accumulate, or additional cooking time will be needed.
5. When cooking time is up, rest the turkey 15 to 20 minutes; temperature should reach 190°F. Return to oven for additional cooking if needed.
6. Garnish with green grapes and serve.

About 2 servings per pound

Note: If desired, turkey cavity may be filled with Apple Dressing. Follow Roast Turkey recipe, but add 6 minutes per pound to the cooking time.

Apple Dressing

1½ cups finely chopped celery
  ⅔ cup finely chopped onion
  1 cup butter
  1 teaspoon salt
  1 teaspoon sage or thyme
  ½ to ¾ cup water
 12 cups dry bread cubes
  3 cups pared and chopped apple

1. In a 3-quart glass casserole, sauté celery and onion in butter 2 to 3 minutes, stirring after every minute.
2. Mix together salt, sage, and water. Pour over bread cubes, tossing lightly to mix.
3. Add bread cubes to vegetable mixture. Stir in apple, blending evenly.
4. Stuff turkey just before roasting, or cook dressing in a 3-quart casserole dish 10 to 12 minutes, rotating dish one-quarter turn halfway through cooking time.
5. Rest 5 minutes before serving.

10 to 12 servings

Note: This dressing is also good with pork chops. Extra dressing may be frozen and reheated later.

Yesterday's Turkey Casserole

¼ **cup butter**
⅓ **cup flour**
½ **cup chopped onion**
¾ **cup thinly sliced celery**
1½ **cups water**
2 **chicken bouillon cubes**
¾ **teaspoon salt**
8 **small fresh mushrooms, sliced**
2 **cups cooked diced turkey**

1. In a 2-quart glass casserole, cook butter 30 to 45 seconds. Add flour; blend until smooth. Stir in onion, celery, water, bouillon cubes, and salt.
2. Cook 5 to 6 minutes, until mixture thickens. Stir once halfway through cooking.
3. Add mushrooms and turkey; stir to blend.
4. Cook, covered, 3 to 4 minutes, rotating dish one-quarter turn halfway through cooking time.
5. Serve over **toast, rice,** or **leftover stuffing.**

4 servings

Note: Chicken may be substituted for turkey. If no leftover cooked chicken is available, cook chicken breasts 7 minutes per pound. Cool chicken, remove meat from bones, and dice.

Turkey Tetrazzini

8 **ounces uncooked spaghetti**
¼ **cup butter**
¼ **cup flour**
1 **teaspoon salt**
¼ **teaspoon nutmeg**
2 **cups turkey broth or 2 chicken bouillon cubes dissolved in 2 cups hot water**
1 **cup evaporated milk**
¼ **cup sherry**
¼ **cup grated Parmesan cheese**
2 **cups cubed cooked turkey or chicken**
¼ **pound green pepper, chopped**
½ **pound fresh mushrooms, sliced**
1 **egg yolk**
½ **cup slivered almonds**

1. Cook spaghetti following package directions. Drain well.
2. In a 4-cup glass measure, heat butter 30 seconds. Blend in flour, salt, and nutmeg. Stir until mixture is smooth.
3. Stir broth and milk into flour mixture. Cook until mixture boils, 6 to 8 minutes, stirring after every minute. Blend sherry and cheese into sauce and add sauce to cooked spaghetti.
4. In a 2-quart glass casserole, combine spaghetti, turkey, green pepper, mushrooms, and egg yolk; blend thoroughly. Sprinkle with almonds.
5. Cook, uncovered, 6 to 8 minutes, rotating dish one-quarter turn halfway through cooking time. Rest 10 minutes before serving.

6 to 8 servings

Conventional oven: Bake at 350°F 25 to 30 minutes.

Chicken Livers and Mushrooms

1 **to 1½ pounds chicken livers**
½ **pound fresh mushrooms, thinly sliced**
¼ **cup grated onion**
2 **tablespoons chopped parsley**
¾ **teaspoon salt**
½ **teaspoon pepper**
½ **cup burgundy**
¼ **cup butter**
6 **slices toast or 3 English muffins, split and toasted**

1. Dice livers coarsely. Combine with mushrooms, onion, parsley, salt, pepper, and wine in a large plastic bag. Marinate in refrigerator overnight.
2. In a 2-quart glass casserole, heat butter 30 to 45 seconds. Add chicken-liver mixture.
3. Cook, uncovered, 6 to 8 minutes, stirring every 2 minutes. Cover casserole and cook 3 to 4 minutes more.
4. Spoon onto toasted bread or muffins arranged on serving platter.

4 to 6 servings

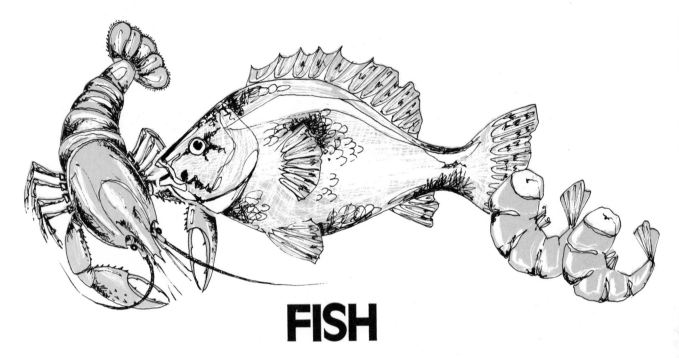

FISH

All seafood cooks very quickly in the microwave and will require about 5 or 6 minutes per pound cooking time. We prefer to cook most fish covered so that it will remain moist and tender. It may be rolled in crackers or bread crumbs which will brown during the cooking time. If fish is your main dish, you may prefer to cook it after cooking the vegetable rather than before, because of the length of time needed for cooking.

A carry-over cooking time of 5 to 10 minutes is needed for fish. We prefer to leave the fish covered during this time so that the center will cook without overcooking the outside edges.

Seafood with a shell, such as lobster and clams, can be cooked in the shell and is a natural for microwave cooking.

Stuffed Flounder

¼ cup chopped green onion
¼ cup butter
1 can (4 ounces) chopped mushrooms
1 can (6½ ounces) crab meat, drained
½ cup cracker crumbs
2 tablespoons parsley flakes
½ teaspoon salt
¼ teaspoon pepper
2 pounds flounder fillets, cut in serving pieces
2 tablespoons butter
2 tablespoons flour
¼ teaspoon salt
Milk
⅓ cup sherry
1 cup shredded Cheddar cheese
½ teaspoon paprika
1 teaspoon parsley flakes

1. In a 2-quart glass casserole, combine green onion and butter and cook 2 to 3 minutes, stirring after every minute.
2. Drain mushrooms and reserve liquid. Combine mushrooms, crab meat, cracker crumbs, 2 tablespoons parsley flakes, salt, and pepper with cooked onion. Spread mixture over fish fillets. Roll up each piece of fish and secure with a wooden pick. Place seam side down in a 10-inch glass baking dish.
3. In a 4-cup glass measure, heat butter 30 seconds. Stir in flour and salt.
4. Add enough milk to reserved mushroom liquid to make 1 cup. Gradually stir milk and sherry into flour mixture. Cook sauce 2 to 3 minutes, stirring every minute, until thickened. Pour sauce over flounder.
5. Cook flounder 6 to 8 minutes, rotating dish one-quarter turn halfway through cooking time.
6. Sprinkle cheese, paprika, and 1 teaspoon parsley flakes over fish. Cook 3 to 5 minutes, or until fish flakes easily with fork.

6 to 8 servings

Fish with Caper Stuffing

1 dressed trout, pike, haddock, perch, or flounder (about 1½ pounds)
1 teaspoon salt
1 cup coarse dry bread crumbs
¼ cup capers
2 tablespoons finely chopped green onion
2 tablespoons finely chopped parsley
1 egg, slightly beaten
2 to 4 tablespoons half-and-half
Lemon wedges

1. Rinse fish under cold water; drain well and pat dry with paper towels. Sprinkle cavity with salt and set aside.
2. Combine bread crumbs, capers, green onion, and parsley. Blend egg with 2 tablespoons half-and-half and pour over bread crumb mixture. Mix until moistened, adding additional half-and-half if necessary.
3. Lightly pile stuffing into fish. Fasten with wooden picks or secure with string. Place in an 11×7-inch baking dish. Cover with waxed paper.
4. Cook fish 8 to 10 minutes, or until fish flakes when tested with a fork; rotate dish one-quarter turn halfway through the cooking time. Allow to stand 2 minutes after cooking before serving. Garnish with lemon wedges.

4 servings

Red Snapper à l'Orange

1 pound red snapper, cut in serving pieces
2 tablespoons orange juice
1 teaspoon grated orange peel
1 tablespoon butter
½ teaspoon lemon juice
½ teaspoon salt
¼ teaspoon pepper
Parsley sprigs

1. In a 2-quart glass baking dish, arrange fish evenly around edge.
2. In a 1-cup glass measure, blend orange juice, orange peel, butter, lemon juice, salt, and pepper. Heat 30 seconds and pour over fish.
3. Cook fish, covered, 5 to 6 minutes, rotating dish one-quarter turn halfway through cooking time.
4. Rest, covered, 5 minutes before serving. Garnish with parsley.

4 servings

Crab-Stuffed Sole

3 tablespoons butter
3 tablespoons flour
1½ cups milk
⅓ cup sherry
½ teaspoon salt
1 cup shredded Swiss cheese
2 pounds sole fillets
Salt
Pepper
1 medium onion, minced

1. In a 4-cup glass measure, heat butter 30 seconds. Stir in flour, milk, sherry, and salt, blending well. Cook 2 to 3 minutes, stirring every minute until thickened. Stir in cheese and set aside.
2. Cut fish in serving pieces and sprinkle with salt and pepper.
3. In a 4-cup glass measure, cook onion in butter 2 to 3 minutes, stirring once, until tender. Add crab meat, mushrooms, and cracker crumbs; mix well.
4. Spread crab meat mixture evenly over each piece of fish.

2 tablespoons butter
1 can (6½ ounces) crab meat
5 fresh mushrooms, cleaned and
    chopped
½ cup cracker crumbs
   Parsley flakes

Roll up pieces of fish and secure with a wooden pick. Place seam side down in a 10-inch glass baking dish.
5. Cook, covered, 5 to 6 minutes, rotating dish one-quarter turn halfway through cooking time. Remove pan drippings and pour sauce over fish. Cook 2 to 3 minutes, sprinkle with parsley flakes, and serve.

6 to 8 servings

Sole Sauté Amandine

3 tablespoons flour
¾ teaspoon salt
¼ teaspoon pepper
1 pound sole or other white fish
   fillets
1 tablespoon oil
¼ cup butter
¼ cup sliced almonds
1 tablespoon fresh lemon juice
1 tablespoon chopped parsley

1. Combine flour, salt, and pepper in a shallow dish. Dip fillets into mixture, coating on all sides.
2. In a 10-inch glass dish, heat oil and 1 tablespoon butter 1 minute. Place fillets in dish and cover.
3. Sauté 4 to 5 minutes, turning fillets over and rotating dish one-quarter turn halfway through cooking time. Rest, covered, 5 minutes.
4. In a 1-cup glass measure, combine 3 tablespoons butter, almonds, and lemon juice. Cook and stir 1 to 2 minutes, until brown.
5. Pour sauce over fillets, sprinkle with parsley, and serve immediately.

3 or 4 servings

Salmonburgers

1 can (16 ounces) salmon
½ cup chopped onion
¼ cup salad oil
⅓ cup dry bread crumbs
2 eggs, beaten
1 teaspoon dry mustard
½ teaspoon salt
½ cup dry bread crumbs

1. Drain salmon, reserving ⅓ cup liquid; set aside.
2. In a 2-cup glass measure, cook onion in oil 2 to 2½ minutes. In a large mixing bowl, combine onion, ⅓ cup dry bread crumbs, reserved salmon liquid, eggs, mustard, salt, and salmon; mix well. Shape into 6 patties.
3. Roll patties in ½ cup bread crumbs. Place on roasting rack in a 2-quart baking dish. Cook patties 5 to 6 minutes, rotating dish one-quarter turn halfway through cooking time. Rest 5 minutes before serving.

3 or 4 servings

Salmon Ring: Follow recipe for Salmonburgers. Form mixture into a ring in a 1½-quart glass baking dish. Place a glass, open end up, in center of ring. Cook 5 to 6 minutes, rotating dish one-quarter turn halfway through cooking time. Rest 5 minutes before serving.

Cold Poached Salmon

2 cups water
½ fresh lemon, thinly sliced
½ medium onion, thinly sliced
6 whole cloves
1 bay leaf
1 stalk celery, cut in 1-inch pieces
1½ teaspoons salt
2 tablespoons lemon juice
3 tablespoons vinegar
4 salmon steaks or fillets

1. In a 2-quart glass baking dish, combine water, lemon, onion, cloves, bay leaf, celery, salt, lemon juice, and vinegar. Heat, covered, 5 to 6 minutes, stirring halfway through cooking time.
2. Arrange salmon in corners of baking dish. Cook, covered, 5 to 6 minutes, rotating dish one-quarter turn halfway through cooking time.
3. Gently turn fish over in liquid and rest, covered, 2 to 3 minutes. Fish should flake easily when tested with a fork. Add more cooking time if desired.
4. Remove fish from liquid. Serve hot or refrigerate 3 to 4 hours and serve cold with tartar sauce.

4 servings

Note: Halibut or other fish fillets may be substituted for the salmon.

Baked Halibut

¼ cup butter
½ teaspoon dry mustard
1½ tablespoons parsley flakes
2 teaspoons lemon juice
¼ teaspoon garlic powder
1 pound halibut fillets, cut in serving pieces

1. In a 10-inch glass baking dish, heat butter 30 seconds. Add mustard, parsley flakes, lemon juice, and garlic powder; stir to blend.
2. Coat fish in sauce and arrange around sides of dish.
3. Cook, covered, 5 to 6 minutes, rotating dish one-quarter turn halfway through cooking time.
4. Rest, covered, 5 minutes before serving.

4 or 5 servings

Microwave Turbot

1 egg, slightly beaten
1 tablespoon lemon juice
½ teaspoon salt
Dash pepper
½ cup corn flake crumbs
1 pound turbot fillets, cut in serving pieces

1. In a small glass bowl, combine egg, lemon juice, salt, and pepper. Dip fish into mixture and coat with crumbs.
2. Arrange fish around edge of a 10-inch baking dish.
3. Cook, covered, 4 to 5 minutes, rotating dish one-quarter turn halfway through cooking time.

4 or 5 servings

Note: Any white fish may be substituted for the turbot.

Paprika Buttered Fish Fillets

1 package (1 pound) frozen fish fillets
 (perch, haddock, cod, or halibut),
 thawed
Flour
Salt and pepper
2 tablespoons butter
Paprika

1. Dip fillets in flour seasoned with salt and pepper; coating well. Set aside.
2. Melt butter in an 11x7-inch baking dish. Dip fillets in butter and arrange in baking dish. Sprinkle with paprika.
3. Cook, uncovered, 2 to 4 minutes. Do not turn fish over, but do rotate dish one-quarter turn halfway through cooking time.
4. Serve garnished with **cooked asparagus spears** and **carrots**.

About 4 servings

Crab Casserole

1 can (10½ ounces) condensed cream
 of mushroom soup
1 pound crab meat
½ cup coarsely chopped walnuts
1 can (5 ounces) water chestnuts,
 drained and sliced
½ cup finely chopped onion
1 cup sliced celery
1 teaspoon Worcestershire sauce
¼ teaspoon Tabasco
4 to 6 small fresh mushrooms,
 cleaned and sliced
1 can (5 ounces) chow mein noodles
1 cup corn flake crumbs

1. In a 2-quart glass baking dish, blend soup, crab meat, walnuts, water chestnuts, onion, celery, Worcestershire sauce, Tabasco, and mushrooms.
2. Stir in noodles and spread mixture evenly in dish. Cover with corn flake crumbs.
3. Cook 10 to 12 minutes, rotating dish one-quarter turn halfway through cooking time.
4. Rest, covered with waxed paper, 5 to 10 minutes before serving.

6 to 8 servings

Conventional oven: Bake at 350°F 30 minutes.

Note: Two cans (6½ or 7 ounces each) tuna or salmon may be substituted for the crab meat.

Shrimp Creole

3 tablespoons butter
½ cup chopped onion
½ cup thin strips green pepper
½ cup diced celery
1 clove garlic, minced
1 can (16 ounces) tomatoes, drained
1 can (8 ounces) tomato sauce
1 tablespoon Worcestershire sauce
1 teaspoon salt
1 teaspoon sugar
½ teaspoon chili powder
 Dash Tabasco
1 tablespoon cornstarch
1 pound cooked shrimp, peeled and
 deveined

1. In a 3-quart glass casserole, blend butter, onion, green pepper, celery, and garlic. Cook 3 to 4 minutes, stirring halfway through cooking time.
2. Stir in tomatoes, tomato sauce, Worcestershire sauce, salt, sugar, chili powder, and Tabasco. Cook 8 minutes, stirring every 3 minutes.
3. In a 1-cup glass measure, blend cornstarch with 2 tablespoons liquid from tomato mixture, and blend into casserole.
4. Cook 3 to 4 minutes, stirring halfway through cooking time. Fold in shrimp and heat 2 to 3 minutes.
5. Rest 10 minutes before serving.

5 or 6 servings

Creamed Scallops

¼ cup butter
¼ cup finely chopped onion
¼ cup flour
6 fresh medium mushrooms, cleaned
  and sliced
¼ cup sherry
½ teaspoon salt
¼ teaspoon pepper
1 pound medium scallops
2 teaspoons lemon juice
½ cup evaporated milk
1 egg yolk
1 tablespoon chopped parsley

1. In a 2-quart glass casserole, heat butter 30 seconds. Add onion and cook until soft, 1 to 2 minutes. Blend in flour.
2. Add mushrooms, sherry, salt, pepper, scallops, and lemon juice; mix well.
3. Cook, covered, 5 to 6 minutes, rotating dish one-quarter turn halfway through cooking time.
4. In a 1-cup glass measure, blend milk with egg yolk, and stir carefully into scallop mixture.
5. Cook, covered, 3 to 4 minutes, stirring halfway through cooking time.
6. Rest 5 minutes. Sprinkle parsley over top and serve.

3 or 4 servings

Nutty Tuna Casserole

1 can (10½ ounces) condensed cream
  of mushroom soup
1 soup can water
1 can (6½ or 7 ounces) tuna, drained
1 cup chopped celery
½ cup chopped onion
½ cup cashews
1 can (5 ounces) chow mein noodles

1. In a 1-quart glass casserole blend soup, water, tuna, celery, onion, and cashews. Sprinkle noodles over top.
2. Cook 10 to 12 minutes, rotating dish one-quarter turn halfway through cooking time.
3. Rest 5 minutes before serving.

4 or 5 servings

Tuna Casserole

2 cans (6½ or 7 ounces each) tuna,
  drained
1 stalk celery, diced
2 eggs
1 cup uncooked oats
1 can (10½ ounces) condensed cream
  of celery soup
1 tablespoon lemon juice
½ teaspoon salt
  Dash pepper
1 package (10 ounces) frozen peas

1. In a 1½-quart glass casserole, combine tuna, celery, eggs, and oats. Add soup, lemon juice, salt, and pepper, mixing well.
2. Cook, covered, 5 to 7 minutes, rotating dish one-quarter turn halfway through cooking time.
3. Pierce frozen pea package and cook 3 minutes in microwave. Drain liquid off peas and fold into casserole.
4. Cook casserole, covered, 3 to 4 minutes. Rest, covered, 10 minutes before serving.

About 6 servings

Conventional oven: Mix all ingredients except peas. Bake at 350°F 50 minutes. Cook peas as directed on package, drain, and fold into casserole just before serving.

MAIN DISHES

Most main dishes will cook in about 10 to 15 minutes for the average casserole (3 or 4 servings). Generally this is the recipe that is cooked first for the meal preparation, as with conventional cooking. Very often the dish can be cooked and served in the same container. It is wise to purchase a few dishes that you would want to place on your table for serving and still use for cooking. The serving dishes with your dinnerware will often meet this need. If you prefer the top of the casserole to be crisp, cover with a crumb topping and do not cover during the cooking time. For a soft texture, cook covered. If you want cheese on the top of a dish, add this near the end of the cooking time.

Lasagna

4 cups water
8 ounces lasagna noodles
1 tablespoon salad oil
1½ pounds ground beef
1 clove garlic, crushed in a garlic press
1 cup small curd cottage cheese
4 ounces mozzarella cheese, shredded
½ teaspoon salt
½ cup mayonnaise
1 jar (16 ounces) spaghetti sauce without meat
½ teaspoon oregano
Grated Parmesan cheese

1. In a large pan on range, bring the water to boiling. Add noodles and salad oil. Cook 5 to 6 minutes until tender; drain.
2. In a medium glass mixing bowl, break apart ground beef. Add garlic and cook 6 to 7 minutes, stirring every 2 minutes. Drain off drippings.
3. Add cottage cheese, mozzarella cheese, salt, and mayonnaise to meat mixture; stir to blend.
4. In a 9-inch glass baking dish, place a layer of noodles on the bottom and cover with a layer of meat mixture. Continue layering with remaining noodles and meat. Pour spaghetti sauce over top and sprinkle with oregano and desired amount of Parmesan cheese.
5. Cook, covered, 6 to 8 minutes, rotating dish one-quarter turn halfway through cooking time.
6. Rest, covered, 10 minutes before serving.

4 to 6 servings

Tortilla Casserole

1½ pounds ground beef
1 medium onion, chopped
1 clove garlic, minced
1 tablespoon chili powder
1 can (15 ounces) tomato sauce
⅔ cup water
8 corn tortillas
2½ cups shredded Cheddar cheese

1. In a 2-quart glass casserole, crumble ground beef and combine with onion and garlic. Cook 5 to 6 minutes, stirring halfway through cooking time.
2. Stir in chili powder, tomato sauce, and water. Cook 3 to 4 minutes, stirring halfway through cooking time.
3. In a 2-quart glass casserole, alternate layers of tortillas, meat sauce, and cheese, reserving ½ cup cheese for the top.
4. Cook, covered, 6 to 8 minutes, rotating dish one-quarter turn halfway through cooking time.

6 to 8 servings

Chili

1 pound ground beef
1 medium onion, diced
2 teaspoons flour
2 cans (16 ounces each) tomatoes (undrained)
2 cans (16 ounces each) kidney beans
1 tablespoon salt
1 to 2 tablespoons chili powder
¼ teaspoon thyme
1 cup water or ketchup

1. In a 3-quart glass casserole, sauté ground beef and onion 6 minutes, stirring every 2 minutes.
2. Mix flour with tomatoes and add to meat mixture. Blend in kidney beans, salt, chili powder, thyme, and water.
3. Cook, covered, 10 to 12 minutes, stirring halfway through cooking time.
4. Rest 5 minutes before serving.

4 to 6 servings

Conventional oven: Bake at 350°F 1 hour.

Quick Beef Pie

1½ pounds ground beef
1 medium onion, finely chopped
½ teaspoon salt
1 can (10½ ounces) condensed tomato soup
1 can (16 ounces) cut green beans, drained
¼ teaspoon pepper
1½ cups seasoned mashed potatoes
½ cup shredded Cheddar cheese

1. In a 10-inch glass dish, crumble beef. Add onion and salt; cook 6 to 7 minutes, stirring halfway through cooking time, until browned. Drain off excess drippings.
2. Add soup, green beans, and pepper to meat mixture. Cook 3 to 4 minutes, stirring halfway through cooking time.
3. Press meat mixture into dish. Drop potatoes in mounds around edge of hot mixture, and sprinkle with cheese.
4. Cook 3 to 4 minutes, rotating dish one-quarter turn halfway through cooking time.
5. Rest 5 minutes before serving.

5 or 6 servings

Conventional oven: Bake at 350°F 25 to 30 minutes.

Note: If desired, the pie may be browned under a conventional broiler, but only if it is in a glass ceramic dish.

Marzetti

1 pound ground beef
1 large onion, diced
½ green pepper, diced
6 to 8 fresh medium mushrooms, cleaned and sliced
1 teaspoon salt
¼ teaspoon pepper
¼ teaspoon oregano
1 can (10½ ounces) condensed tomato soup
1 can (6 ounces) tomato paste
⅓ cup water
1 tablespoon Worcestershire sauce
4 ounces noodles, cooked
8 ounces Cheddar cheese, shredded

1. In a 2-quart glass casserole, cook ground beef, onion, and green pepper 4 to 6 minutes, stirring twice. Add mushrooms, salt, pepper, and oregano; stir to blend.
2. In a mixing bowl, combine soup, tomato paste, water, and Worcestershire sauce.
3. In a 2-quart glass casserole dish, place a layer of noodles, then a layer of meat, cover with half the sauce, and half the cheese. Repeat layering, ending with cheese.
4. Cook 12 to 15 minutes, rotating dish one-quarter turn halfway through cooking time.
5. Rest casserole 10 minutes before cutting and serving.

6 to 8 servings

Conventional oven: Bake at 375°F 45 minutes.

Hacienda Casserole

1 cup chopped onion
1 pound ground beef
½ pound bulk pork sausage
1 can (16 ounces) corn, drained
1 can (10½ ounces) condensed tomato soup
1 can (6 ounces) tomato paste
1 can (16 ounces) chili with beans, drained
¾ teaspoon salt
¼ teaspoon pepper
2 cups shredded Cheddar cheese
1 pound noodles, cooked

1. In a 2-quart glass casserole, brown onion, ground beef, and sausage 4 to 6 minutes. Remove excess drippings.
2. Add corn, soup, tomato paste, chili, salt, and pepper. Stir to blend evenly.
3. In a 10-inch glass skillet, layer half the meat mixture, half the noodles, and 1 cup cheese; repeat with remaining ingredients.
4. Cook 10 to 12 minutes, rotating dish one-quarter turn halfway through cooking time.

6 to 8 servings

Conventional oven: Bake at 350°F 45 minutes.

Italian Casserole

8 ounces (about 4 cups) fettucine
1 pound bulk pork sausage
¼ cup chopped onion
1 can (4 ounces) sliced mushrooms
2 tablespoons chopped pimento-stuffed olives
2 cups (about 8 ounces) shredded Cheddar cheese
1 can (8 ounces) enchilada sauce
2 tablespoons shredded Cheddar cheese

1. Cook fettucine as directed on package. Drain well.
2. In a 2-quart glass casserole, cook sausage and onion 5 to 6 minutes, stirring every 2 minutes. Drain well.
3. Drain mushrooms, reserving ¼ cup liquid. In a mixing bowl, toss together fettucine, sausage, onion, mushrooms with liquid, olives, 2 cups cheese, and enchilada sauce. Turn into a 2-quart glass casserole.
4. Cook 10 to 12 minutes, rotating dish one-quarter turn halfway through cooking time.
5. Sprinkle 2 tablespoons cheese over top and cook an additional minute.

5 or 6 servings

Conventional oven: Bake at 375°F 30 to 35 minutes.

Macaroni-Franks Dinner

8 ounces macaroni
1 pound frankfurters, cut in 1-inch
   pieces
1 cup mayonnaise
2 ounces Cheddar cheese, cut in thin
   strips
½ cup sliced green onion
2 tablespoons prepared mustard
½ teaspoon salt
¼ teaspoon pepper

1. Cook macaroni as directed on package. Drain well.
2. In a 1½-quart casserole, combine frankfurters, mayonnaise, cheese, green onion, mustard, salt, and pepper; stir to blend. Stir in cooked macaroni.
3. Cook, covered, 6 to 8 minutes, rotating dish one-quarter turn halfway through cooking time.
4. Rest 5 minutes before serving.

6 to 8 servings

Macaroni in Cheese Sauce

3 cups macaroni
¼ cup butter
¼ cup flour
½ teaspoon salt
2 cups milk
½ teaspoon dry mustard
1½ cups shredded Cheddar cheese

1. Cook macaroni as directed on package.
2. In a 1½-quart glass casserole, heat butter 30 seconds. Stir in flour and salt. Add milk slowly, stirring continuously.
3. Cook 4 to 5 minutes until mixture thickens. Add mustard and cheese; stir to blend. Cook 1 minute.
4. Mix in cooked macaroni and heat 2 to 3 minutes.

5 or 6 servings

Shrimp Tetrazzini

8 ounces thin spaghetti
2 tablespoons butter
1 medium onion, chopped
8 ounces cooked shrimp, peeled and
   deveined
8 ounces fresh mushrooms, cleaned
   and sliced
¼ cup flour
¼ cup mayonnaise
1 teaspoon salt
1½ cups milk
¼ cup sherry
   Parmesan cheese, grated

1. Cook spaghetti as directed on package. Drain well.
2. In a 1½-quart glass casserole, heat butter 30 seconds. Add onion and cook 2 to 3 minutes, stirring halfway through cooking time.
3. Stir in shrimp and mushrooms. Cook 4 to 6 minutes, stirring halfway through cooking time.
4. In a 4-cup glass measure, blend flour, mayonnaise, and salt. Stir in milk and sherry. Cook 3 to 4 minutes, stirring every minute until thickened. Add spaghetti and sauce to shrimp mixture; blend well. Sprinkle cheese over top.
5. Cook 8 to 10 minutes, rotating dish one-quarter turn halfway through cooking time.
6. Rest, covered, 10 minutes.

4 or 5 servings

Dinner Special

2 tablespoons bacon drippings
½ cup flour
2 cups milk
2 cups shredded Cheddar cheese
1 can (16 ounces) green beans, drained
1 can (16 ounces) luncheon meat, cut in ½-inch chunks
3 cups cooked rice

1. In a 4-cup glass measure, heat drippings 30 seconds. Stir in flour. Slowly stir in milk, blending well.
2. Cook until boiling, 3 to 4 minutes.
3. In a 2-quart glass casserole, combine cheese, green beans, and luncheon meat. Blend with sauce. Stir in rice.
4. Cook 5 to 7 minutes, rotating dish one-quarter turn halfway through cooking time.
5. Rest 10 minutes before serving.

5 or 6 servings

Fish and Rice

1½ cups packaged precooked rice
¼ cup chopped onion
1 teaspoon salt
1 tablespoon parsley flakes
¼ teaspoon poultry seasoning
2 tablespoons lemon juice
1¼ cups water
1 pound fresh whitefish fillets, cut in serving pieces
2 tablespoons butter
   Paprika

1. In a 2-quart glass casserole, blend rice, onion, salt, parsley flakes, poultry seasoning, lemon juice, and water. Spread mixture evenly in casserole.
2. Arrange fillets over rice mixture, dot with butter, and sprinkle evenly with paprika.
3. Cook, covered, 10 to 12 minutes, rotating dish one-quarter turn halfway through cooking time.
4. Rest, covered, 5 minutes and serve hot.

4 or 5 servings

Texas Hash

1 pound ground beef
2 large onions, sliced
2 medium green peppers, chopped
½ cup chopped celery
2 cans (16 ounces each) tomatoes
¾ cup rice
½ teaspoon salt
   Pepper to taste

1. In a 3-quart glass baking dish, cook crumbled ground beef 5 minutes, stirring halfway through cooking time. Spoon off drippings.
2. Add onion, green pepper, celery, tomatoes, rice, salt, and pepper; stir to blend.
3. Cook, covered, 20 minutes, rotating dish one-quarter turn halfway through cooking time.
4. Rest, covered, 10 minutes before serving.

4 to 6 servings

Ground Beef and Wild Rice Casserole

1 **pound ground beef**
½ **cup diced onion**
½ **cup uncooked wild rice**
1 **cup water**
1 **can (10½ ounces) condensed cream**
  of chicken soup
1 **can (10½ ounces) condensed cream**
  of mushroom soup
5 **fresh mushrooms, cleaned and**
  chopped
1 **cup slivered blanched almonds**
½ **cup butter**
1 **cup water**
1 **package (8 ounces) stuffing cubes**

1. In a 2-quart glass casserole, cook crumbled ground beef 3 to 4 minutes, stirring halfway through cooking time. Drain off drippings.
2. Add onion, wild rice, and 1 cup water to ground beef; stir to mix. Cook 3 minutes, rotating dish one-quarter turn halfway through cooking time.
3. Add chicken soup, mushroom soup, mushrooms, and almonds to ground beef mixture; stir to blend evenly.
4. In a 2-quart glass mixing bowl, heat butter until melted, about 45 seconds. Stir in 1 cup water and stuffing cubes, blending well.
5. Spoon stuffing mix over meat mixture. Cook 14 to 16 minutes, rotating dish one-quarter turn halfway through cooking time.
6. Rest 10 minutes before serving. Invert on a serving platter, or serve from casserole.

4 to 6 servings

Note: If long grain rice is substituted for wild rice, reduce final cooking time about 3 minutes.

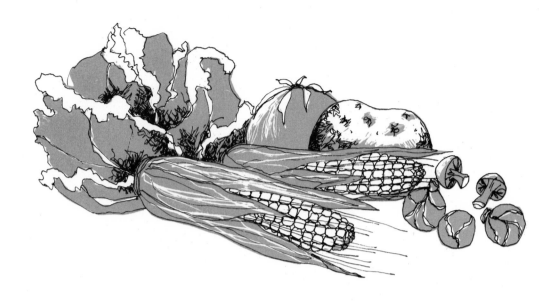

VEGETABLES AND SALADS

The color, flavor, and texture of vegetables cooked in the microwave are generally superior to most other methods of conventional cooking. If the vegetable has a natural skin cover, such as potatoes, squash, or corn on the cob, this will be the container and it isn't necessary to dirty a dish. Place the food on a roasting rack in the bottom of the oven for cooking. Other vegetables should be cooked covered. The vegetables should be stirred or rotated halfway through the cooking time. A carry-over cooking time of 5 to 10 minutes is needed before serving. The foods should remain covered during this time.

Many vegetables will seem to be a little firm when removed from the oven but will continue to cook. If you prefer your vegetables with a softer texture they can be cooked longer; however, we find children prefer the crisp texture of microwave-cooked vegetables.

Seasonings can be added during the cooking time with the exception of salt, which will distort the cooking pattern and cause drying of the vegetable. Add salt at or near the end of the cooking time.

Frozen vegetables can be cooked in the carton. Remove the wrap from one end of a paper carton or pierce the plastic bag prior to cooking. Allow 6 or 7 minutes per pound cooking time. It is not necessary to defrost the vegetables prior to cooking.

When preparing fresh vegetables, wash them prior to placing in a dish. The water clinging to the vegetable is all that is needed for cooking most vegetables. Arrange the vegetable for the best cooking pattern if it has a specific shape, keeping in mind the doughnut cooking shape that will occur with microwave cooking. With broccoli and asparagus, place the stalk end near the outside of the container and the flower end near the center of the dish.

Canned vegetables have been cooked so need only reheating in the microwave. Remove most of the liquid from the vegetable before heating. Heat and serve in the same container.

The microwave will not be used much for making salads because most of the salads we eat are made from fresh ingredients. It does work very well for gelatin salads or those served wilted or warm. The microwave is also great for preparing the ingredients needed for a salad, such as potatoes, bacon, or cooked eggs. If you have a favorite cooked salad dressing, it can be prepared with ease in the microwave using the technique we use for sauces—"cook and stir."

FRESH VEGETABLE COOKING CHART

Rotate dish one-quarter turn or stir halfway through cooking time.
Rest, covered, 5 minutes before serving. Season as desired.

VEGETABLE	AMOUNT	COOKING TIME	INSTRUCTIONS
Artichoke	1 medium (4 inches in diameter)	6–7 minutes	Wash thoroughly, allowing a small amount of water to cling to leaves. Wrap in waxed paper and place on glass pie plate (or small glass dish). Rotate dish as directed.
Asparagus (fresh cut or spears)	15 stalks (¾ pound)	6–7 minutes per pound	Pop white portion off bottom of each spear. Wash thoroughly, allowing a small amount of water to cling to spears. Arrange in glass loaf dish with approximately one half the stalks pointing each way. Cook, covered. Rotate dish as directed.
Beans			
Butter	1 pound	6–8 minutes per pound	Wash thoroughly. Put ½ cup water in 1-quart casserole. Add beans and cook, covered. Stir as directed.
Green or Wax	3 cups (1 pound)	6–7 minutes per pound	Wash thoroughly. Add ¼ cup water to 1½-quart glass dish. Salt, if desired, and add beans to dish. Cook, covered, stirring as directed.
Lima	1 pound	6–8 minutes per pound	Wash thoroughly. Add ½ cup water and ½ teaspoon salt to 1-quart glass dish. Add beans and cook, covered. Stir as directed.
Pinto	1 pound	20–25 minutes per pound	Soak beans overnight. Add 3 cups water to 2-quart casserole. Add beans and cook, covered. Stir as directed.
Beets	4 medium (whole)	15–17 minutes	Clean beets. Place in 2-quart glass dish. Cover beets with water and cook, covered, stirring as directed.
Broccoli	1 small bunch (1 pound)	6–7 minutes per pound	Wash stalks and split to uniform size. Add ¼ cup water and ½ teaspoon salt, if desired, to 2-quart glass dish. Arrange broccoli with stems along outside of dish. Cook covered. Rotate dish as directed.
Brussels Sprouts	1 tub (10 ounces)	6–7 minutes per pound	Wash and remove dried leaves. Add 2 tablespoons water and ½ teaspoon salt, if desired, to 1-quart glass dish. Add sprouts to dish and cook, covered. Rotate dish as directed.

VEGETABLE	AMOUNT	COOKING TIME	INSTRUCTIONS
Cabbage	1 small head (1 pound)	6–7 minutes per pound	Wash and shred, or cut in wedges. Add 2 tablespoons water and ½ teaspoon salt, if desired, to 1½-quart glass dish. Add cabbage and cook, covered. Rotate dish as directed.
Carrots	6 whole medium (1 pound)	7–8 minutes per pound	Pare and wash carrots. Slice in equal rounds, dice, or cut lengthwise in even strips. Add ¼ cup water and ½ teaspoon salt, if desired, to 1½-quart glass dish. Add carrots and cook, covered. Stir as directed.
Cauliflower	1 small head (1 pound)	6–7 minutes per pound	Wash and trim. Leave whole or trim flowerets from stem. Add 2 tablespoons water and ½ teaspoon salt, if desired, to 1½-quart glass dish. Add cauliflower and cook, covered. If left whole, rotate dish as directed. If cut in flowerets, stir as directed.
Celery	3 cups sliced (1 pound)	6–7 minutes per pound	Wash and slice. Add 2 tablespoons water and ½ teaspoon salt, if desired, to 1½-quart glass dish. Add celery and cook, covered. Stir as directed.
Corn (cut from the cob)	2 cups (¾ pound)	6–7 minutes per pound	Shuck ears and cut corn off cob. Add 2 tablespoons water or cream and ½ teaspoon salt, if desired, to 1-quart glass dish. Add corn and cook, covered, stirring as directed.
Corn (on the cob)	1 medium ear (approximately ¾ pound)	2–3 minutes	Pull back husks to check condition of corn. Remove husks except for about 2 layers, leaving silk in place. (The husks will serve as the container to trap steam when cooking corn.) Arrange corn evenly on oven shelf and cook. Remove husks and silks with clean hot pads. Dip corn in butter, if desired.
	2 ears	4–5 minutes	Note: Corn may be husked and silked before cooking. Wrap in waxed paper or place in a covered glass dish and cook. Rotate dish as directed.
	3 ears	5–6 minutes	
	4 ears	6–7 minutes	
	5 ears	7–8 minutes	
	6 ears	8–9 minutes	
	8 ears	10–12 minutes	

VEGETABLE	AMOUNT	COOKING TIME	INSTRUCTIONS
Cucumbers	2 medium (¾ pound)	6–7 minutes per pound	Pare and dice in ½-inch cubes. Add 2 tablespoons water or cream and ½ teaspoon salt, if desired, to 1-quart glass dish. Add cucumbers and cook, covered, stirring as directed.
Eggplant	1 small (1 pound)	6–7 minutes per pound	Pare and dice in ½-inch cubes. Add 2 tablespoons water and ½ teaspoon salt, if desired, to 1½-quart glass dish. Add eggplant and cook, covered, stirring as directed.
Greens (beet, chard, collard, dandelion, kale, mustard, spinach, and turnip)	4 cups (1 pound)	6–7 minutes	Wash and cook, covered, in water that clings to leaves in 2-quart glass dish. Rotate dish as directed.
Mushrooms	For garnish	1–2 minutes	Because mushrooms are porous, they cook very quickly. It is best to weigh for most accurate cooking time. Clean, slice, and cook in 1-quart covered glass dish. 1 to 2 tablespoons butter may be added, if desired. Stir as directed.
	1 pound	4 minutes	
Onions	8 small or 2 large (1 pound)	6–7 minutes per pound	Clean and quarter or slice onions. Place in 1-quart glass dish and cook, covered. Rotate dish as directed. Season or add sauce.
Parsnips	4 medium (1 pound)	7–8 minutes per pound	Split, remove core if desired, and wash. Add ¼ cup water and ½ teaspoon salt, if desired, to 1½-quart glass dish. Add parsnips and cook, covered. Rotate dish as directed.
Peas Black-Eye			These are best cooked from the dry stage conventionally. After cooking, they may be reheated in the microwave.
Green	1 cup (1 pound)	5 minutes per pound	Shell peas. Add 2 tablespoons water and 2 teaspoons salt, if desired, to 1-quart glass dish. Add peas and cook, covered, stirring as directed.
Pods (or Snow Peas)			Same cooking directions as above.

VEGETABLE	AMOUNT	COOKING TIME	INSTRUCTIONS
Peppers Green or Red	2 large (1 pound)	6–7 minutes per pound	Cut core from peppers and clean, allowing some water to cling to peppers. Arrange evenly in 2-quart glass dish and cook, covered. Rotate dish as directed.
Potatoes (baked)	2 small or 1 large (1 pound)	6–7 minutes per pound	Potatoes should be even in size and shape. After scrubbing, pierce the skins to allow steam to escape. Arrange potatoes 1 inch apart in a circle on oven shelf and cook. Rearrange potatoes and turn over halfway through cooking time. For convenience, potatoes may be placed on a dish or rack and the dish rotated. Remove potatoes from microwave when fork comes out with a little resistance.
	1 medium	3½–4 minutes	
	2 medium	6½–7 minutes	
	3 medium	8½–9 minutes	
	4 medium	10–11 minutes	
	5 medium	13–14 minutes	
	6 medium	15–16 minutes	
	8 medium	21–23 minutes	
Potatoes (boiled)	2 medium	8–10 minutes	Pare and quarter potatoes, keeping pieces in a uniform size if possible. In 1½-quart glass dish, add 1½ cups water and 1 teaspoon salt, if desired. Add potatoes, cover, and cook. (Cooking time can be reduced by boiling water prior to cooking.) Note: You may find it more convenient to boil potatoes on the surface of your range. About the same time is required for more than 4 potatoes.
	4 medium	15–18 minutes	
Potatoes Sweet or Yams	1 medium	3–4 minutes	Potatoes should be even in size and shape. After scrubbing, pierce the skins to allow steam to escape. Arrange potatoes 1 inch apart in a circle on oven shelf and cook. Rearrange potatoes and turn over halfway through cooking time. For convenience, potatoes may be placed on a dish or rack and the dish rotated as directed. Remove potatoes from microwave when fork comes out with a little resistance.
	2 medium	5–6 minutes	
	4 medium	7–8 minutes	
	6 medium	8–9 minutes	
Pumpkin			Same as for Hubbard Squash.

VEGETABLE	AMOUNT	COOKING TIME	INSTRUCTIONS
Squash Acorn, Butternut, or Danish	1 small (1 pound)	6–8 minutes	Pierce squash and place whole on dish or rack. Cook, rotating as directed and turning over. When done, cut in half and remove seeds.
	2 small	12–14 minutes	
Hubbard	6×6-inch piece (1 pound)	6–7 minutes per pound	Wash, leaving about ¼ cup water on squash. Wrap in waxed paper and place on glass dish. Cook. Turn over and rotate dish as directed. Note: Squash may be cut into 1-inch cubes. (Precook 1 to 2 minutes to make cutting easier.) Add ¼ cup water and 1 teaspoon salt to 1½-quart glass dish. Add squash, cover, and cook. Rotate dish as directed.
Zucchini	2 medium (1 pound)	6–7 minutes per pound	Wash and slice ¼-inch thick. Add ¼ cup water and ½ teaspoon salt to 1-quart glass dish. Add zucchini, cover and cook. Note: Pierce and cook whole, if desired. Skin may be left on squash to add color and texture.
Tomatoes	4 medium (1 pound)	6 minutes	Wash and core firm ripe tomatoes. Arrange evenly in 2-quart glass dish. Cover and cook. Caution: Be careful to avoid over-cooking tomatoes. They can lose their shape and become juicy when heated too long.
Turnips	2 medium (1 pound)	6–7 minutes	Wash and cut in eighths. Add ¼ cup water and ½ teaspoon salt, if desired, to 1½-quart glass dish. Add turnips and cook, covered. Rotate dish as directed.

Fresh Vegetable Tips

—These cooking times are as close to correct as possible. You will have some variation depending on the texture, freshness, and shape of each vegetable. Weight is the most accurate measure of cooking time, and practice is the best teacher to avoid overcooking!

—Many of these vegetables will be crisp-tender, as some people prefer. If you prefer a softer texture, cook the vegetable 1 to 2 minutes longer. Always rest before adding more cooking time!

—It is not recommended to wrap whole vegetables such as potatoes and squash in foil at the end of the cooking time, because this traps moisture between the foil and the vegetable and can make it soggy. It would be better to wrap in terry cloth to absorb some of the moisture, and at the same time help to keep the heat in the potato. If potatoes must be held for longer periods of time, reheat in the microwave before serving.

—Leave the lid on the container during resting unless the recipe suggests removing it.

FROZEN VEGETABLE COOKING CHART

Rotate plate or dish one-quarter turn halfway through
cooking time. Rest 5 minutes. Season and serve.

VEGETABLE	AMOUNT	COOKING TIME	INSTRUCTIONS
Artichoke Hearts	10-ounce package	4–5 minutes	Slash or pierce package. Cook in package placed on paper plate. Or, cook artichokes with 2 tablespoons water in 1-quart glass covered casserole.
Asparagus (spears or pieces)	10-ounce package	6–8 minutes	Slash or pierce package. Cook in package placed on paper plate. Or, cook asparagus with 2 tablespoons water in 1-quart glass covered casserole. For 9-ounce pouch, place pouch in a glass dish and make slash in the top. Cook 5 to 6 minutes.
	2 (10-ounce) packages	9–10 minutes	
	3 (10-ounce) packages	12–14 minutes	
Beans Green or Wax	10-ounce package (carton or pouch)	6–8 minutes	Slash or pierce package. Cook in package placed on paper plate. Or, cook beans with 2 tablespoons water in 1-quart glass covered casserole.
	2 (10-ounce) packages	11–13 minutes	
	3 (10-ounce) packages	14–16 minutes	
Lima	10-ounce package (carton or pouch)	9–10 minutes	Cook beans with ⅓ cup hot water in 1½-quart glass covered casserole. Rotate dish or stir halfway through cooking time.
	2 (10-ounce) packages	14–16 minutes	
	3 (10-ounce) packages	18–20 minutes	
Broccoli (chopped or spears)	10-ounce package (carton or pouch)	6–8 minutes	Slash or pierce package. Cook in package placed on paper plate. Or, cook broccoli in 1-quart glass covered casserole.
	2 (10-ounce) packages	8–10 minutes	
Brussels Sprouts	10-ounce package (carton or pouch)	6–8 minutes	Slash or pierce package. Cook in package placed on paper plate. Or, place Brussels sprouts and 2 tablespoons water in 1-quart glass covered casserole. Cook.
	2 (10-ounce) packages	8–10 minutes	
	3 (10-ounce) packages	11–13 minutes	

VEGETABLE	AMOUNT	COOKING TIME	INSTRUCTIONS
Carrots (diced)	10-ounce package (carton or pouch)	6–8 minutes	Slash or pierce package. Cook in package placed on paper plate. Or, cook carrots in 1-quart glass covered casserole.
Cauliflower	10-ounce package (carton or pouch)	6–8 minutes	Slash or pierce package. Cook in package placed on paper plate. Or, cook cauliflower in 1-quart glass covered casserole.
	2 (10-ounce) packages	8–10 minutes	
	3 (10-ounce) packages	11–13 minutes	
Corn (cut from the cob)	10-ounce package (carton or pouch)	4–6 minutes	Slash or pierce package. Cook corn with 2 tablespoons water in 1-quart glass covered casserole.
	2 (10-ounce) packages	6–8 minutes	
	3 (10-ounce) packages	8–10 minutes	
Corn (on the cob)	1 ear	4–6 minutes	Defrost frozen corn on the cob in the refrigerator overnight. Wrap in waxed paper or place in 2-quart glass covered casserole; cook.
	2 ears	6–8 minutes	
	3 ears	8–10 minutes	
	4 ears	10–12 minutes	
Mixed Vegetables	10-ounce package (carton or pouch)	5–7 minutes	Slash or pierce package. Cook in package placed on paper plate. Or, cook vegetables with 2 tablespoons water in 1-quart glass covered casserole.
	2 (10-ounce) packages	8–10 minutes	
	3 (10-ounce) packages	11–13 minutes	
Onions (frozen in cream sauce)	10-ounce package (carton or pouch)	5–7 minutes	Slash or pierce package. Cook in package placed on paper plate. Or, cook onions in 1-quart glass covered casserole.
	2 (10-ounce) packages	8–10 minutes	
	3 (10-ounce) packages	11–13 minutes	
(frozen chopped)			These can be defrosted in the microwave in a matter of minutes for use in recipes.

Roast Turkey, 43;
Cranberry Sauce, 18

VEGETABLE	AMOUNT	COOKING TIME	INSTRUCTIONS
Peas and Carrots	10-ounce package (carton or pouch)	4–6 minutes	Slash or pierce package. Cook in package placed on paper plate. Or, cook peas and carrots in 1-quart glass covered casserole.
	2 (10-ounce) packages	6–8 minutes	
	3 (10-ounce) packages	8–10 minutes	
Peas Black-eye	10-ounce package	10–12 minutes	Cook peas with ¼ cup hot water in 1-quart glass covered casserole. Stir halfway through cooking time.
	2 (10-ounce) packages	15–16 minutes	
Green	10-ounce package (carton or pouch)	4–6 minutes	Slash or pierce package. Cook in package placed on paper plate. Or, cook peas in 1-quart glass covered casserole.
Pods (or Snow Peas)	10-ounce package	4–6 minutes	Slash or pierce package. Cook in package placed on paper plate. Or, cook peas in 1-quart glass covered casserole.
	2 (10-ounce) packages	7–9 minutes	
Spinach (leaf or chopped)	10-ounce package (carton or pouch)	4–6 minutes	Slash or pierce package. Cook in package placed on paper plate. Or, cook spinach in 1-quart glass covered casserole.
	2 (10-ounce) packages	7–9 minutes	
	3 (10-ounce) packages	10–12 minutes	
Squash Hubbard	10-ounce package	5–7 minutes	Cook squash in 1-quart glass covered casserole.
	2 (10-ounce) packages	8–10 minutes	
	3 (10-ounce) packages	10–12 minutes	

Paprika Buttered Fish Fillets, 49

Frozen Vegetable Tips

—You can speed up the cooking time of frozen vegetables if you remove them from the freezer at the start of the meal preparation. At room temperature, they will require less cooking time.

—It is recommended to place the frozen carton on a paper plate because the dyes from some packages will stain the bottom of your oven.

—Cooking in the freezing pouches works very well. Each pouch must be slashed prior to cooking to allow steam to escape.

—Use your microwave as a convenience in freezing vegetables. Select vegetables freshly picked. Heat in the microwave to blanch, then chill in cold water; drain. Pack and freeze immediately. The cooking times may vary but are usually one third the cooking time for the fresh vegetable. You eliminate saturating the vegetable with hot water.

—Package leftovers and freeze for later use. Glass or heat-proof plastic containers are best.

—If you plan to cook a bulky food that has been frozen, defrost first in the microwave.

Canned Vegetable Tips

—Remove the liquid from canned vegetables prior to heating in the microwave. (They heat faster without it.) You may want to save the juices for soups or sauces.

—Canned vegetables have already been cooked; therefore, heating, not cooking, is required before serving. Most canned vegetables heat in 2 minutes per cup, rotating one-quarter turn or stirring halfway through cooking time.

—Canned vegetables should be covered during the heating time. Use waxed paper, napkin, paper towel, or an inverted saucer.

—A glass measuring cup makes an ideal utensil for heating vegetables.

—Soup is heated in the same manner as canned vegetables. Soup must be stirred about every 45 seconds when heating or it becomes too hot on the exposed surfaces and creates an eruption in the center. You may want to cover with a napkin. Mugs make an ideal utensil for heating soup. They are also easier for children to manage.

—Dried beans and peas cook better conventionally. You may want to substitute canned beans and peas in recipes in the microwave.

—If desired, you may place 1 to 2 tablespoons butter on top of the canned vegetable prior to heating, or you may add it at the end of the cooking time.

Artichokes

Fresh artichokes

1. Slice off about 1 inch from top of artichoke. Cut off stem about 1 inch from base so artichoke will sit upright. Remove tough outside leaves. With scissors, clip tips of remaining leaves. Wash well.
2. Arrange artichokes upright in a glass baking dish. Cover and cook as follows: for 1 artichoke, 6 to 8 minutes; for 2, 12 to 15 minutes; for 4, 20 to 25 minutes.
3. Rest, covered, 10 minutes before serving. Serve with **lemon butter, hollandaise sauce, melted butter,** or **mayonnaise.**

Note: Artichokes may be chilled after resting and served cold.

Asparagus Amandine

2 packages (10 ounces each) frozen asparagus
¼ cup finely chopped almonds
¼ cup butter
1 teaspoon wine vinegar

1. Pierce asparagus packages with fork. Cook 6 to 8 minutes, rotating one-quarter turn halfway through cooking time.
2. In a 3-cup glass measure, combine almonds and butter. Cook 1 to 2 minutes, stirring halfway through cooking time. Stir in vinegar.
3. Drain asparagus well and arrange in a 10-inch glass baking

dish. Pour sauce over asparagus and cook, covered, 1 to 2 minutes.

4. Rest, covered, 5 minutes before serving.

4 to 6 servings

Note: If desired, serve cold on lettuce leaves as a salad.

Tangy Pork and Beans

2 cans (16 ounces each) pork and
    beans, drained
½ cup minced onion
1 cup dry white wine
½ cup firmly packed dark brown
    sugar
½ cup honey
1 teaspoon finely crushed bay leaf
1 teaspoon pepper
¼ teaspoon Tabasco

1. In a 2-quart glass casserole, combine pork and beans, onion, wine, brown sugar, honey, bay leaf, pepper, and Tabasco.

2. Cook, covered, 10 to 12 minutes, stirring halfway through cooking time.

3. Rest, covered, 5 minutes before serving.

6 to 8 servings

Creamed Green Beans

1 jar (8 ounces) pasteurized process
    cheese spread
1 can (10½ ounces) condensed cream
    of mushroom soup
    Tabasco
1 tablespoon soy sauce
1 medium onion, chopped
3 tablespoons butter
5 fresh mushrooms, cleaned and
    chopped
1 can (8 ounces) water chestnuts,
    drained and sliced
2 cans (16 ounces each) French-style
    green beans, drained
    Slivered almonds

1. In a 4-cup glass measure, blend cheese spread, soup, Tabasco, and soy sauce. Cook 3 to 5 minutes, stirring halfway through cooking time.

2. In a 1½-quart glass casserole, cook onion and butter 3 to 4 minutes, stirring halfway through cooking time until onions are transparent. Stir in mushrooms and water chestnuts and cook 1 minute.

3. Add green beans and soup mixture to mushroom mixture; stir to blend. Garnish with almonds.

4. Cook 5 minutes, rotating dish one-quarter turn halfway through cooking time.

5. Rest 5 minutes before serving.

6 to 8 servings

Sweet-and-Sour Beets

2 tablespoons brown sugar
1 tablespoon cornstarch
¼ teaspoon salt
1 can (8 ounces) pineapple tidbits
    (undrained)
1 tablespoon butter
1 tablespoon lemon juice
1 can (16 ounces) sliced beets,
    drained

1. In a 1-quart glass casserole, combine brown sugar, cornstarch, and salt. Stir in pineapple with its juice.

2. Cook 3 to 4 minutes, stirring after every minute, until mixture thickens.

3. Add butter, lemon juice, and beets. Cook, covered, 4 to 5 minutes, stirring halfway through cooking time.

4. Rest, covered, 5 minutes.

4 or 5 servings

Easy Broccoli Casserole

2 packages (10 ounces each) frozen
    broccoli spears
1 can (10½ ounces) condensed cream
    of mushroom soup
1 cup crushed potato chips or
    French-fried onion rings
½ cup grated Cheddar cheese

1. Pierce broccoli packages with fork. Cook broccoli 7 to 9 minutes, rotating dish one-quarter turn halfway through cooking time. Rest 5 minutes.
2. Place drained broccoli in a 2-quart glass casserole. Gently stir in soup. Sprinkle potato chips and cheese on top.
3. Cook, covered, 2 to 3 minutes. Remove cover and cook an additional 2 minutes. Serve immediately.

5 or 6 servings

Brussels Sprouts with Buttered Chestnuts

2 packages (10 ounces each) frozen
    Brussels sprouts
1 tablespoon finely chopped onion
⅔ cup sliced cooked chestnuts (see
    Note)
½ teaspoon salt

1. Pierce Brussels sprouts packages with fork. Cook 6 to 8 minutes, rotating one-quarter turn halfway through cooking.
2. In a 1-quart glass casserole, heat butter 30 seconds. Stir in onion, chestnuts, and salt, Cook 3 to 4 minutes, stirring halfway through cooking time.
3. Drain Brussels sprouts and combine with chestnut mixture. Cook, covered, 3 to 4 minutes.
4. Rest, covered, 5 minutes before serving.

6 to 8 servings

Note: To cook chestnuts, slash each chestnut crosswise through skin on flat end of shell. In a glass pie plate, arrange 20 to 24 chestnuts in an even layer. Cook 3 to 4 minutes, stirring every minute, until nuts are soft when squeezed. Rest 5 minutes. Peel off shells and use as directed.

Sweet-and-Sour Cabbage

1 small onion, chopped
3 tablespoons butter
1 cup meat stock or water
1 small head cabbage, shredded
1 small tart apple, cored and diced
3 tablespoons vinegar
1 tablespoon brown sugar
¼ teaspoon allspice
½ teaspoon salt

1. In a 2-quart glass casserole, sauté onion in butter 2 minutes, stirring after 1 minute. Stir in stock, cabbage, and apple.
2. Cover casserole and cook 6 to 8 minutes, stirring halfway through cooking time.
3. Add vinegar, brown sugar, allspice, and salt to cabbage; mix well. Cook 3 to 4 minutes.
4. Rest, covered, 5 minutes before serving.

4 to 6 servings

Cabbage au Gratin

1 medium head cabbage, shredded
2 tablespoons butter
2 tablespoons flour
½ teaspoon salt
1 cup milk

1. In a 3-quart glass casserole, cook cabbage, covered, 10 to 12 minutes, rotating dish one-quarter turn halfway through cooking time. Rest, covered, 5 minutes while preparing sauce.
2. In a 2-cup glass measure, heat butter 30 seconds. Stir in flour and salt; stir until smooth. Add milk gradually, stirring

¾ cup shredded Cheddar cheese
¼ teaspoon dry mustard
Dash paprika

constantly. Cook 2 to 3 minutes, stirring after every minute until mixture boils.
3. Blend in cheese, dry mustard, and paprika. Cook 1 minute and stir well.
4. Drain liquid from cabbage. Add cheese sauce and stir to blend.
5. Rest, covered, 5 minutes before serving.

6 to 8 servings

Orange-Glazed Carrots

6 to 8 medium carrots, pared and
diagonally sliced
2 tablespoons butter
¼ cup brown sugar
2 tablespoons orange juice
1 teaspoon grated orange peel
1 teaspoon lemon juice
¼ teaspoon salt

1. In a 1½-quart glass casserole, combine carrots, butter, brown sugar, orange juice, orange peel, lemon juice, and salt.
2. Cover carrots and cook 10 to 12 minutes, stirring halfway through cooking time.
3. Rest, covered, 10 minutes before serving.

6 to 8 servings

Cauliflower au Gratin

½ cup butter
1 medium head cauliflower, cut in
flowerets
¼ teaspoon garlic salt
¼ teaspoon salt
¼ teaspoon pepper
2 large tomatoes, cut in wedges
¼ cup seasoned bread crumbs
¼ cup grated Parmesan cheese
½ cup shredded Swiss cheese

1. In a 1½-quart glass casserole, heat butter 30 seconds. Add cauliflower, garlic salt, salt, and pepper, and stir to coat cauliflower with butter.
2. Cover cauliflower and cook 5 to 6 minutes, rotating dish one-quarter turn halfway through cooking time.
3. Arrange tomatoes on top of cauliflower and cook 2 minutes.
4. Add bread crumbs, Parmesan cheese, and Swiss cheese. Cook 1 to 2 minutes until cheese begins to melt.
5. Rest, covered, 5 minutes before serving.

3 or 4 servings

Sautéed Celery and Tomatoes

2 tablespoons butter
6 cups diagonally cut celery (½-inch
slices)
½ pound cherry tomatoes, stems
removed
½ teaspoon basil
½ teaspoon salt
¼ teaspoon pepper

1. In a 2-quart glass casserole, heat butter 30 seconds. Stir in celery. Cover and cook 10 to 12 minutes, stirring halfway through cooking time.
2. Stir tomatoes, basil, salt, and pepper into celery. Cook, covered, 3 to 4 minutes.
3. Rest, covered, 5 minutes before serving.

4 to 6 servings

Creamed Corn Casserole

2 tablespoons butter
1 egg
⅓ cup soda cracker crumbs
1 can (17 ounces) cream-style corn
½ teaspoon salt
¼ teaspoon pepper

1. In a 1-quart glass casserole, heat butter 30 seconds. Add egg, cracker crumbs, corn, salt, and pepper; blend evenly.
2. Cook 4 to 6 minutes, stirring halfway through cooking time.
3. Rest 5 minutes before serving.

4 or 5 servings

Eggplant Casserole

1 eggplant (about 1½ pounds)
Salt
Flour
½ cup salad oil for skillet
2 cans (8 ounces each) tomato sauce
1 cup thinly sliced mozzarella cheese
½ cup grated Parmesan cheese

1. Peel eggplant and cut in ½-inch-thick slices. Sprinkle both sides with salt, and set aside 20 to 30 minutes.
2. Dip eggplant slices in flour. Brown eggplant in hot microwave browning dish or in hot salad oil in hot skillet on a conventional range. Drain slices on paper towel.
3. Pour 1 can tomato sauce in a 10-inch glass baking dish. Lay eggplant slices in sauce, and cover with other can of sauce. Place mozzarella cheese over the sauce and sprinkle Parmesan cheese on top.
4. Cover with waxed paper or lid. Cook 12 to 14 minutes, rotating dish one-quarter turn halfway through cooking time.
5. Rest, covered, 5 minutes.

4 to 6 servings

Sautéed Mushrooms

2 tablespoons butter
¼ teaspoon tarragon
½ pound fresh mushrooms, cleaned
and sliced
3 tablespoons chopped green onion
Salt
Pepper

1. In a 1-quart glass casserole, heat butter and tarragon 30 seconds, until butter is melted. Stir in mushrooms, cover, and cook 2 minutes.
2. Add green onion and stir to blend. Cook 3 to 4 minutes, stirring halfway through cooking time. Season with salt and pepper.
3. Rest, covered, 5 minutes before serving.

4 servings

Mustard Greens and Bacon

4 slices bacon, diced
¼ cup finely chopped onion
¾ pound mustard greens
Salt and pepper

1. In a 3-quart glass casserole, cook bacon 2 to 3 minutes, stirring halfway through cooking time.
2. Stir in onion and cover. Cook 3 to 4 minutes, stirring halfway through cooking time, until bacon is crisp. Pour off all drippings, except 1½ tablespoons.
3. Rinse and coarsely chop the mustard greens. Stir the greens into onion mixture, coating them with the drippings.
4. Cover the casserole and cook 2 to 3 minutes. Season with salt and pepper to taste.
5. Rest, covered, 5 minutes before serving.

3 or 4 servings

Note: Fresh spinach may be substituted for mustard greens.

Cooked Onions

1½ pounds small white onions
2 tablespoons butter
1 teaspoon minced sage leaves
½ teaspoon salt

1. In a 1½-quart glass casserole, combine onions, butter, sage, and salt.
2. Cook, covered, 8 to 10 minutes, stirring twice during cooking time.
3. Rest, covered, 5 minutes before serving.

4 servings

Snow Peas with Water Chestnuts

1 tablespoon salad oil or bacon
    drippings
1 can (5 ounces) water chestnuts,
    drained and sliced
½ pound fresh (or 1 10-ounce
    package frozen) snow peas
1 cup water
1 chicken bouillon cube
1 tablespoon cornstarch
2 tablespoons cold water

1. In a 1½-quart glass casserole, heat oil 15 seconds. Add water chestnuts and snow peas.
2. In a 1-cup glass measure, heat water 2 minutes. Dissolve bouillon cube and add to vegetable mixture.
3. Cook vegetables, covered, 4 to 6 minutes, stirring once halfway through cooking time.
4. Combine cornstarch and cold water; mix well. Push vegetables to one side of casserole and stir cornstarch mixture into broth.
5. Stir vegetables into sauce. Cook 2 to 4 minutes, stirring every minute, until sauce is slightly thickened. Salt to taste.

4 servings

Herbed Peas

2 packages (10 ounces each) frozen
    peas
¼ cup butter
½ cup minced onion
¼ cup minced celery
½ cup minced parsley
¼ teaspoon crushed rosemary
¼ teaspoon basil
¾ teaspoon salt

1. Pierce pea packages with fork and cook 6 to 8 minutes, rotating one-quarter turn halfway through cooking time.
2. In a 1½-quart glass casserole, heat butter 30 seconds. Stir in onion and celery. Cook 3 to 4 minutes, stirring halfway through cooking time. Add parsley, rosemary, basil, salt, and drained peas; stir to blend.
3. Cook, covered, 3 to 4 minutes, rotating dish one-quarter turn halfway through cooking time.
4. Rest, covered, 5 minutes.

6 to 8 servings

Cheesy Potato Casserole

1 package (12 ounces) frozen
    shredded hash brown potatoes
1 cup shredded Cheddar cheese
1 tablespoon flour
¼ cup chopped onion
1 teaspoon salt
¼ teaspoon pepper
1 tablespoon dried chives

1. Pierce hash brown potato package. Cook the potatoes 3 to 4 minutes, rotating one-quarter turn halfway through cooking time.
2. In a 2-quart glass casserole, blend hash brown potatoes, cheese, flour, onion, salt, pepper, and chives.
3. Cook, covered, 6 to 8 minutes, rotating dish one-quarter turn halfway through cooking time.
4. Rest, covered, 5 minutes.

4 servings

Scalloped Potatoes

4 medium potatoes, pared and
    thinly sliced
2 tablespoons flour
1½ teaspoons salt
½ cup finely chopped onion
1½ cups milk or evaporated milk
1 tablespoon butter
½ cup shredded sharp Cheddar
    cheese
    Paprika or parsley flakes

1. Arrange sliced potatoes in a buttered 2½-quart glass casserole. Sprinkle flour, salt, and onion over potatoes; mix lightly. Stir in milk and dot with butter.
2. Cook, covered, 15 to 18 minutes, stirring every 4 minutes.
3. Rest, covered, 5 minutes. Sprinkle cheese evenly over top and garnish with paprika or parsley flakes.

4 to 6 servings

Note: Potatoes may be placed under conventional broiler for about 1 minute to brown cheese, but only if casserole dish is glass ceramic material.

Parsleyed Potatoes

¼ cup butter
1 tablespoon lemon juice
½ teaspoon salt
1½ pounds new potatoes, pared and
   cut in serving pieces
3 tablespoons parsley flakes

1. In a 1-cup glass measure, combine butter, lemon juice, and salt. Cook 30 to 45 seconds to melt butter; stir to blend.
2. Arrange potatoes in a 2-quart glass casserole. Pour butter mixture over potatoes, coating evenly. Sprinkle with parsley flakes.
3. Cook, covered, 10 to 12 minutes, rotating dish one-quarter turn halfway through cooking time.
4. Rest, covered, 10 minutes before serving.

4 to 6 servings

Microwave Fried Potatoes

2 tablespoons butter
½ teaspoon salt
⅓ cup corn flake crumbs
3 medium potatoes, pared and sliced
   ½ inch thick
   Paprika

1. In a 1-cup glass measure, heat butter 30 seconds.
2. Combine salt and corn flake crumbs in small paper sack. Shake potato slices in sack to coat each slice with crumbs. Arrange slices in a 9-inch glass baking dish. Pour melted butter evenly over top. Sprinkle with paprika.
3. Cook potatoes, covered, 6 minutes. Remove cover, rotate dish one-quarter turn, and cook, uncovered, 4 to 5 minutes.
4. Rest, uncovered, 5 minutes before serving.

3 or 4 servings

Potato Cheese Boats

4 medium baking potatoes
⅓ cup shredded sharp Cheddar
   cheese
¼ cup finely chopped onion
½ cup dairy sour cream
1 teaspoon salt

1. Bake potatoes about 12 to 14 minutes (6 to 7 minutes per pound), rotating one-quarter turn halfway through cooking time. Test to see if done.
2. In a small mixing bowl, blend cheese, onion, sour cream, and salt.
3. Slice off a top from each cooked potato and scoop out inside. Add potato to cheese mixture and blend well.
4. Stuff potato mixture in potato shells. Cook 1 minute before serving.

4 servings

Sweet Potato Casserole

8 freshly cooked or canned sweet
   potatoes, sliced ½ inch thick
¾ cup orange juice
½ cup brown sugar
½ cup butter
¼ cup hot water
1 tablespoon cornstarch

1. Layer sweet potato slices in a 3-quart glass casserole.
2. In a 2-cup glass measure, blend orange juice, brown sugar, butter, hot water, and cornstarch. Cook 1½ to 2 minutes, stirring every 30 seconds. Pour sauce over sweet potatoes.
3. Cover the sweet potatoes and cook 12 to 15 minutes, rotating dish one-quarter turn halfway through cooking.
4. Rest, covered, 10 minutes.

6 to 8 servings

Conventional oven: Bake, covered, at 375°F 50 to 55 minutes.

Succotash Medley

1 small onion, chopped
¼ cup thinly sliced green pepper
2 cups freshly cooked corn
1 can (16 ounces) lima beans, drained
1 medium zucchini, scrubbed and sliced ¼ inch thick
¼ cup butter
2 teaspoons sugar
1 teaspoon salt
¼ teaspoon pepper
½ teaspoon basil
1 large tomato, cut in thin wedges

1. In a 2-quart glass casserole, combine onion and green pepper. Cook, covered, 2 to 3 minutes, stirring halfway through cooking time.
2. Add corn, lima beans, zucchini, butter, sugar, salt, pepper, and basil; stir to blend. Cook, covered, 8 to 10 minutes, stirring halfway through cooking time.
3. Arrange tomato wedges on top and cook, covered, 2 to 3 minutes to heat tomato.
4. Rest, covered, 5 minutes before serving.

4 to 6 servings

Spinach and Broccoli au Gratin

1 package (10 ounces) frozen chopped broccoli
2 pounds fresh spinach
3 tablespoons butter
3 tablespoons flour
½ teaspoon salt
1½ cups milk
¼ teaspoon pepper
⅓ cup grated Parmesan cheese

1. Pierce broccoli package. Cook broccoli 4 minutes, rotating one-quarter turn halfway through cooking time. Drain well.
2. Wash spinach, remove tough stems, and tear into small pieces. Drain on paper towel. Place spinach in 2-quart glass casserole. Cook 6 to 8 minutes, stirring halfway through cooking time. Drain well.
3. In a 2-cup glass measure, heat butter 30 seconds. Add flour and salt; stir until blended. Blend in milk and cook 3 to 4 minutes, stirring after every minute.
4. Add broccoli and sauce to spinach; stir to blend. Stir in cheese. Cook, covered, 6 to 8 minutes, stirring halfway through cooking time.

6 to 8 servings

Spinach Pudding

2 packages (10 ounces each) frozen chopped spinach
1½ cups cottage cheese, drained
¾ teaspoon salt
¼ teaspoon Tabasco
½ cup grated Parmesan cheese
2 eggs, slightly beaten

1. Pierce spinach packages. Cook spinach 6 to 8 minutes, rotating dish one-quarter turn halfway through cooking time. Drain well.
2. In a 1-quart glass casserole, combine spinach, cottage cheese, salt, Tabasco, Parmesan cheese, and eggs.
3. Cook 5 to 6 minutes, rotating dish one-quarter turn halfway through cooking time, until mixture sets.
4. Rest 5 minutes before serving.

6 to 8 servings

Note: Frozen chopped broccoli may be substituted for the spinach.

Baked Butternut Squash

1 butternut squash (about 2 pounds)
2 tablespoons water
¼ cup butter
½ teaspoon salt
¼ teaspoon pepper

1. Pare squash, cut in ½-inch-thick slices, and remove seeds. Arrange slices in a 2-quart glass baking dish. Sprinkle water over squash and dot with butter.
2. Cook, covered, 10 to 12 minutes, stirring halfway through cooking time. Add salt and pepper; stir to blend.
3. Rest, covered, 5 minutes before serving.

6 servings

Sweetened Acorn Squash

2 medium acorn squash
1 apple, peeled and chopped
2 tablespoons honey
2 tablespoons butter
½ teaspoon salt

1. Wash each squash and pierce with a fork. Place on glass plate or roasting rack. Cook 12 to 14 minutes, turning over and rotating one-quarter halfway through cooking time. Rest 5 minutes.
2. Cut in half lengthwise and remove seeds. Arrange, cut side up, in an 8-inch square glass baking dish. In center of each squash, spoon one-quarter of the apple, ½ tablespoon honey, ½ tablespoon butter, and dash salt.
3. Cover dish with waxed paper. Cook 4 to 6 minutes, rotating dish one-quarter turn halfway through cooking time.
4. Rest 5 minutes before serving.

4 servings

Note: If desired, remove squash and filling from squash shells, mix together, and serve.

Spinach-Stuffed Tomatoes

1 package (10 ounces) frozen chopped spinach
6 slices bacon, diced
6 medium tomatoes
¾ cup bread crumbs
½ teaspoon salt
¼ teaspoon pepper
6 tablespoons dairy sour cream
    Dill weed

1. Pierce spinach package with fork. Cook 4 to 5 minutes, rotating one-quarter turn halfway through cooking time; drain.
2. In a 1-quart glass casserole, cook bacon 4 to 5 minutes, stirring twice during cooking time. With slotted spoon, remove crisp bacon from drippings.
3. Cut a thin slice from top of each tomato and scoop out center. Turn tomatoes over to drain.
4. Combine spinach, bread crumbs, bacon, salt, and pepper. Stuff tomatoes with spinach mixture and arrange near sides of a 9-inch glass baking dish.
5. Cook 5 to 6 minutes, rotating dish one-quarter turn halfway through cooking time.
6. Top each tomato with 1 tablespoon sour cream and a sprinkle of dill weed.

6 servings

Tomato Combo

2 medium sweet green peppers, cut in 1-inch pieces
1 medium onion, sliced ¼ inch thick
1 can (28 ounces) whole tomatoes, drained
½ teaspoon basil
1 teaspoon salt

1. In a 1-quart glass casserole, spread green pepper pieces evenly over bottom. Separate onion slices and arrange on top of green pepper. Combine tomatoes, basil, and salt. Stir to blend lightly and pour over onion slices.
2. Cook, covered, 10 to 12 minutes, rotating dish one-quarter turn halfway through cooking time.
3. Rest, covered, 5 minutes before serving.

4 to 6 servings

Breaded Tomatoes

2 tablespoons butter
1 small onion, finely chopped
3 slices white bread, cut in ½-inch cubes
1 can (28 ounces) tomatoes (undrained)

1. In a 1½-quart glass casserole, cook butter and onion 2 to 3 minutes, stirring halfway through cooking time. Add bread cubes and stir to coat with butter.
2. Cook 2 to 3 minutes, stirring halfway through cooking time, until bread is lightly toasted. Remove half the bread cubes. Add tomatoes with juice, sugar, salt, basil, and pepper;

1 tablespoon sugar
¼ teaspoon salt
¼ teaspoon basil
¼ teaspoon pepper

stir to blend. Sprinkle remaining bread cubes over top.
3. Cook 5 to 6 minutes, rotating dish one-quarter turn half-way through cooking time.

5 or 6 servings

Lemony Turnips and Carrots

3 cups diced pared turnips
2 cups diced pared carrots
¼ cup water
½ teaspoon salt
2 tablespoons butter
1 tablespoon lemon juice
2 tablespoons chopped parsley

1. In a 2-quart glass casserole, combine turnips and carrots and pour the water over all. Cook, covered, 12 to 15 minutes, stirring every 5 minutes; drain.
2. Stir in salt, butter, and lemon juice. Cook, covered, 2 minutes.
3. Rest, covered, 5 minutes. Sprinkle with parsley before serving.

4 to 6 servings

Zucchini Bake

½ pound zucchini, sliced ¼ inch thick
1 green onion (including top), chopped
2 tablespoons butter
3 eggs
½ cup milk
1 teaspoon salt
¼ teaspoon pepper
¼ teaspoon thyme
1 cup shredded mozzarella cheese

1. In a 9-inch glass cake dish, blend zucchini, onion, and butter. Cover and cook 3 to 4 minutes, rotating dish one-quarter turn halfway through cooking time.
2. Blend eggs, milk, salt, pepper, and thyme; pour over hot zucchini. Cook, covered, 4 to 6 minutes, rotating dish one-quarter turn halfway through cooking time.
3. Sprinkle cheese over top and cook 1 minute to melt cheese. If a glass ceramic baking dish is used, the zucchini may be placed under a conventional broiler for a minute or two.
4. Rest 5 to 6 minutes. Cut in wedges or squares to serve.

4 or 5 servings

Note: For an appetizer, cut Zucchini Bake in bite-size pieces.

Vegetable Casserole

1 package (10 ounces) frozen peas and carrots
1 package (10 ounces) frozen corn
1 teaspoon salt
2 tablespoons butter
1 tablespoon dried mint leaves

1. In a covered 2-quart glass casserole, cook frozen vegetables 6 to 7 minutes, rotating dish one-quarter turn halfway through cooking time.
2. Add salt, butter, and mint leaves; stir to blend. Cover and cook 2 to 3 minutes.
3. Rest 5 minutes before serving.

6 servings
Conventional oven: Bake, covered, at 375°F 50 to 55 minutes.

Spinach and Mushroom Salad

4 slices cooked bacon (page 38)
1 pound fresh spinach
2 hard-cooked eggs, finely chopped
½ pound fresh mushrooms, cleaned and sliced
2 teaspoons grated orange peel
⅔ cup orange juice
1 tablespoon lemon juice
⅓ cup bacon drippings
2 tablespoons soy sauce
½ teaspoon garlic powder

1. Crumble bacon into small pieces.
2. Wash spinach and remove tough stems. Dry with paper towel. Tear leaves into bite-size pieces and arrange in salad bowl.
3. Add eggs, mushrooms, and bacon. Cover tightly and refrigerate until serving time.
4. In a 1-quart glass measure, blend orange peel, orange juice, lemon juice, bacon drippings, soy sauce, and garlic powder. Cook 1 to 2 minutes, stirring every 30 seconds, until mixture boils.
5. Pour hot dressing over spinach just prior to serving.

4 to 6 servings

Fresh Vegetable Medley

1 pound broccoli, cut in thin stalks
1 small head cauliflower (about 1 pound), cut in flowerets
1 large zucchini, sliced ¼ inch thick
1 large crookneck squash, sliced ¼ inch thick
1 large pattypan squash, sliced ¼ inch thick
5 or 6 fresh mushrooms, cleaned and cut in half
1 medium sweet red pepper, cut in strips
1 medium sweet green pepper, cut in strips
¼ cup butter
½ teaspoon garlic salt
¼ teaspoon pepper

1. In a 2-quart glass baking dish or on a large glass serving platter, arrange broccoli around edge of dish; place cauliflower next to broccoli, and squash, mushrooms, and peppers alternately near the center of the dish.
2. In a 1-cup glass measure, combine butter, garlic salt, and pepper; heat 30 to 45 seconds. Drizzle butter over vegetables.
3. Cook, covered, 15 to 20 minutes or until vegetables are done as desired, rotating dish one-quarter turn every 5 minutes.
4. Rest, covered, 5 minutes before serving.

10 to 12 servings

Mexican Salad

1 pound ground beef
¼ cup chopped onion
1 can (16 ounces) kidney beans, drained
½ cup French dressing
¼ cup water
1 tablespoon chili powder
4 cups shredded lettuce
½ cup sliced green onion
2 cups shredded sharp Cheddar cheese
Lettuce leaves for lining salad bowl

1. In a 2-quart glass casserole, sauté ground beef and onion 4 to 6 minutes, stirring twice.
2. Stir in kidney beans, French dressing, water, and chili powder. Cook 4 to 6 minutes, stirring halfway through cooking time.
3. In a large mixing bowl, combine lettuce and green onion. Add meat sauce and 1½ cups cheese; toss lightly. Arrange in lettuce-lined serving bowl and sprinkle with remaining ½ cup cheese.
4. Serve hot or cold with crisp **corn chips.**

4 to 6 servings

German Potato Salad

4 medium potatoes
4 to 6 slices bacon, diced
2 tablespoons flour
¼ cup sugar
1½ teaspoons salt
½ teaspoon celery seed
¼ teaspoon pepper
1 cup water
½ cup vinegar

1. Clean and pierce potatoes with fork. Arrange in a circle on a glass plate or roasting rack, and cook 12 to 15 minutes, rotating plate and turning potatoes over halfway through cooking time.
2. In a 2-quart glass casserole, cook bacon, covered with paper towel, 4 to 6 minutes, stirring halfway through cooking time. Remove crisp bacon from drippings, crumble, and set aside.
3. Stir flour, sugar, salt, celery seed, and pepper into bacon drippings. Cook 1 to 2 minutes, stirring halfway through cooking time.
4. Add water and vinegar to flour mixture. Cook until boiling, about 2 to 3 minutes, stirring every minute.
5. Peel potatoes and cut into ½-inch cubes. Stir potatoes and bacon into sauce. Cover and heat 2 minutes.
6. Rest, covered, 10 minutes before serving.

6 to 8 servings

Frosted Lime Salad

1 cup water
1 package (3 ounces) lime-flavored gelatin
1 can (8 ounces) crushed pineapple
1 cup small curd cottage cheese
½ cup finely diced celery
½ cup chopped walnuts
1 package (3 ounces) cream cheese
1 tablespoon mayonnaise
1 teaspoon lemon juice

1. In a 1-cup glass measure, heat water 2½ to 3 minutes, to boiling.
2. In a medium mixing bowl, dissolve gelatin in boiling water. Chill until thickened but not set, about 20 minutes.
3. Stir in pineapple, cottage cheese, celery, and walnuts. Pour into mold and chill until firm.
4. In a 2-cup glass measure, heat cream cheese about 15 seconds. Add mayonnaise and lemon juice; beat until smooth.
5. Unmold firm gelatin and spread with cream cheese mixture.

6 to 8 servings

Party Fruit Salad

1 can (20 ounces) pineapple chunks, drained, reserving 2 tablespoons juice
1 can (17 ounces) Royal Ann cherries, pitted and drained
1 can (11 ounces) mandarin oranges, drained
2 cups seedless grapes
1 large apple, pared, cored, and diced
2 cups miniature marshmallows
2 eggs
2 tablespoons sugar
2 tablespoons pineapple juice
2 tablespoons brandy or rosé wine
½ teaspoon dry mustard
½ cup dairy sour cream

1. In a large salad bowl, combine pineapple chunks, cherries, orange sections, grapes, apple, and marshmallows. Chill until serving time.
2. In a 2-cup glass measure, combine eggs, sugar, pineapple juice, brandy, and dry mustard. Stir with wire whip to blend well. Cook 2 to 3 minutes, stirring every 30 seconds, until mixture thickens and is light. Cool.
3. Drain excess liquid from fruit. Fold cooled dressing and sour cream into fruit until evenly blended. Chill until serving time.

8 to 10 servings

Cooked Salad Dressing

1 tablespoon butter
1 tablespoon flour
1 tablespoon prepared mustard
¼ teaspoon salt
½ cup sugar
½ cup vinegar
1 egg, beaten

1. In a 2-cup glass measure, heat butter 15 seconds. Add flour, mustard, and salt; blend well. Stir in sugar, and slowly blend in vinegar and egg.
2. Cook 2 to 3 minutes, stirring after every minute, until mixture becomes very thick. Cool and chill before using.

About 1 cup

Note: If desired, thin the dressing with fruit juice to serve on a fruit salad.

Molded Crab Salad

1 cup water
1 package (3 ounces) lemon-flavored gelatin
½ cup diced green pepper
½ cup diced onion
½ cup diced celery
1 cup cooked crab meat
¾ cup condensed tomato soup
3 ounces cream cheese, softened
1 cup mayonnaise

1. In a 2-cup glass measure, heat water and gelatin 2½ to 3 minutes, until mixture boils, stirring once halfway through cooking time. Cool about 20 minutes.
2. Add green pepper, onion, celery, and crab meat; stir to blend. Stir in tomato soup, cream cheese, and mayonnaise.
3. Pour into oiled mold and refrigerate about 2 hours, until firm.
4. Unmold to serve.

8 to 10 servings

Molded Fruit Salad

⅔ cup pineapple juice
⅓ cup water
1 package (3 ounces) lemon-flavored gelatin
1 cup well-drained canned pineapple chunks
¼ cup lemon juice
¼ cup chopped walnuts
2 tablespoons chopped maraschino cherries
¼ teaspoon salt
1 cup chopped unpared apple
1 cup whipping cream, whipped

1. In a 2-cup glass measure, combine pineapple juice and water and heat to boiling, about 2½ to 3 minutes.
2. Dissolve gelatin in hot mixture. Chill until thickened and syrupy, about 20 minutes.
3. Combine pineapple chunks, lemon juice, walnuts, cherries, salt, and apple in mixing bowl. Fold in whipped cream and thickened gelatin mixture.
4. Chill about 2 hours until firm.

6 to 8 servings

Seafoam Salad

1 package (3 ounces) lime-flavored gelatin
¾ cup boiling water
Dash salt
1 cup diced cucumber, drained
2 tablespoons lemon juice
1 teaspoon minced onion
1 cup dairy sour cream

1. In a 2-cup glass measure, combine gelatin and water. Heat until boiling, about 1½ to 2 minutes, stirring halfway through cooking time. Add salt and chill until slightly thickened, about 20 minutes.
2. Stir in cucumber, lemon juice, and onion. Fold in sour cream until marbled effect is produced.
3. Pour into mold. Chill.
4. Umold when ready to serve.

4 or 5 servings

DESSERTS AND BEVERAGES

Cooked desserts of practically all types—cakes, cookies, puddings, pies—can be easily cooked in your microwave oven with delicious results. Microwave cakes are moist and tender. They do not brown as a conventionally baked cake does, but the addition of a topping or icing easily remedies that. Bar cookies are especially easy to prepare in the microwave, and puddings cook very evenly if stirred frequently to distribute the energy. Pie crusts cooked the microwave way are tender and flaky; a two-crust pie can be browned in a conventional oven after the microwave baking.

Beverages are a versatile food when cooked in the microwave. It is usually more convenient to cook them in smaller quantities than large. Very large quantities can probably be cooked faster and more efficiently on the conventional range. One of the most convenient uses of the microwave is to heat one cup of coffee, tea, or cocoa. Or when making a pot of coffee, cups may be reheated as needed in the microwave. If the beverage has a milk base, it may boil over more quickly than those without, because the fat content in the milk speeds up the cooking time.

If you want the liquid to boil, select a large container. If your oven has several speeds, you may want to reduce the energy to achieve a simmer. Stir small amounts at the end of the cooking time to distribute the heat evenly. Large amounts will need stirring halfway through the cooking time. Beverages can be cooked or heated faster by covering during the cooking.

Carrot Cake

1¾ cups all-purpose flour
1 cup sugar
1 teaspoon baking powder
1 teaspoon baking soda
½ teaspoon salt
½ teaspoon cinnamon
½ teaspoon nutmeg
2 eggs
1 cup salad oil
½ cup orange juice
1 teaspoon vanilla extract
1 cup grated carrots
1 cup coarsely chopped walnuts
   Hard Sauce (page 80) (optional)

1. In a large mixing bowl, combine all ingredients except nuts and sauce. Beat 2 minutes until evenly blended. Fold in walnuts.
2. Pour batter into a 10-inch glass dish. Cook 6 to 8 minutes, rotating dish one-quarter turn every 2 minutes.
3. Rest 10 minutes before cutting. Frost with Hard Sauce, if desired.

12 to 16 servings

Note: Cake may bake more evenly with a glass, open end up, in center of dish.

Hard Sauce

2 tablespoons butter
1 cup sifted confectioners' sugar
1 to 2 tablespoons rum or brandy
    Dash salt

1. In a 2-cup glass measure, combine butter, confectioners' sugar, rum, and salt.
2. Cook 1 minute, stirring after 30 seconds. Serve hot or cold.

1½ cups

Cake-Mix Layer Cake

1 package (about 18½ ounces) cake mix

1. Prepare cake mix as directed on package, reducing the liquid by one-quarter the amount called for in mixing instructions.
2. Line bottoms of two 8-inch glass baking dishes with paper towel. Pour batter into baking dishes, filling no more than half full. Save extra batter and make cupcakes. Rest batter 10 minutes, if desired.
3. Cook, one layer at a time, 5 to 6 minutes, rotating dish one-quarter turn halfway through cooking time. When wooden pick stuck in center comes out slightly moist, cake is done.
4. Rest each layer 5 minutes before removing from dish. Cool completely before frosting.

Two 8-inch cake layers

Note: Square baking dishes hold more batter than round and will require 2 to 3 minutes more cooking time per pan.

Cake-Mix Sheet Cake: Follow recipe for Cake-Mix Layer Cake. Pour batter into an 11×7-inch glass baking dish, filling no more than half full. Cook 9 to 11 minutes, rotating one-quarter turn twice during cooking time. If cake begins to overcook in corners, shield with small pieces of foil. Cool 5 minutes before removing from dish; or cake may be left in dish. Frost when completely cool.

Apricot Almond Upside-Down Cake

⅓ cup butter
½ cup firmly packed brown sugar
1 can (16 ounces) apricot halves
½ cup blanched almonds, slivered
2 eggs
⅔ cup sugar
1 teaspoon almond extract
1 cup all-purpose flour
½ teaspoon baking powder
¼ teaspoon salt

1. In a 9-inch glass dish, heat butter 30 to 45 seconds. Blend with brown sugar and spread evenly over bottom of pan. Drain apricots and reserve juice. Arrange almonds and apricot halves over sugar mixture.
2. In a medium mixing bowl, beat eggs until thick. Using an electric mixer, beat about 5 minutes on high speed. Gradually add sugar. Add 6 tablespoons liquid from apricots and almond extract; beat well.
3. Add flour, baking powder, and salt to egg mixture; beat until well blended. Pour over fruit.
4. Cook 5 to 6 minutes, rotating dish one-quarter turn halfway through cooking time.
5. Rest 5 minutes, invert onto serving dish, and serve.

6 to 8 servings

Cupcakes

Prepared cake batter

1. Line glass custard cups, drinking cups, or cupcaker with paper baking cups. Pour 3 tablespoons batter into each cup.
2. Arrange cups in a circle on a glass plate, if not using cupcaker. Cook as follows, rotating plate or cupcaker one-quarter turn halfway through cooking time: 1 cupcake, 10 to 20 seconds; 2 cupcakes, 30 to 45 seconds; 3 cupcakes, 45 to 60 seconds; 4 cupcakes, 1 to 1¼ minutes; and 6 cupcakes, 1½ to 2 minutes.

Date Cake

Cake:
- 2 cups boiling water
- ½ cup chopped dates
- 2 teaspoons baking soda
- 1 cup butter
- 2 cups sugar
- 2 eggs
- 3 cups all-purpose flour
- 2 teaspoons vanilla extract
- 1 teaspoon salt

Topping:
- 3 tablespoons butter
- 1 cup brown sugar
- ¼ cup milk or cream
- 1 cup coarsely chopped walnuts

1. In a 4-cup glass measure, heat water about 5 to 6 minutes, to boiling. Stir in dates and sprinkle baking soda over water. Cool until just warm.
2. Cream butter with sugar and eggs. Add flour, vanilla extract, and salt to creamed mixture. Blend with date mixture and pour into a buttered 2-quart glass ceramic baking dish.
3. Cook 9 to 11 minutes, rotating dish one-quarter turn every 3 minutes.
4. Rest 5 minutes before removing from dish.
5. To make topping, heat butter 30 seconds in a 2-cup glass measure. Add brown sugar, milk, and nuts. Blend ingredients evenly and spread on top of cake.
6. Place cake under conventional broiler 1 to 2 minutes, until mixture starts to bubble. Remove and serve warm.

20 to 24 servings

Conventional oven: Bake at 350°F 45 minutes.

Apple Cake

Cake:
- 1½ cups all-purpose flour
- ¾ teaspoon baking soda
- ¾ teaspoon nutmeg
- ½ teaspoon salt
- ¼ cup salad oil
- ¾ cup sugar
- 1 egg, beaten
- 3 tablespoons buttermilk
- 1½ cups diced pared apples

Topping:
- 3 tablespoons butter, softened
- ⅓ cup firmly packed brown sugar
- 2 tablespoons milk or cream
- ¼ teaspoon vanilla extract
- ½ cup shredded coconut

1. Sift together flour, soda, nutmeg, and salt; set aside. Cream oil with sugar; beat until light and fluffy. Blend in egg.
2. Add buttermilk and flour mixture alternately to creamed mixture. Beat 2 minutes until smooth. Fold in apples.
3. Pour batter into a buttered 8-inch square glass ceramic baking dish. Cook 5 to 7 minutes, rotating dish one-quarter turn halfway through cooking time. Rest 5 minutes before removing from pan.
4. To make topping, heat butter 30 seconds in a 2-cup glass measure. Add brown sugar, milk, vanilla extract, and coconut. Stir to blend ingredients.
5. Spread evenly over top of cake and place under conventional broiler 1 to 2 minutes, until mixture starts to bubble. Remove and serve warm.

9 to 12 servings

Conventional oven: Bake at 350°F 45 minutes.

Poppy Seed Ring Cake

1 package (18½ ounces) prepared
    yellow cake mix
1 package (3¾ ounces) lemon instant
    pudding and pie filling
4 eggs
½ cup cooking oil
1 cup water
⅓ cup poppy seed
  Butter
  Sugar

1. In a large mixing bowl, combine cake mix, pudding and pie filling, eggs, oil, water, and poppy seed. Beat mixture at low speed of electric mixer until ingredients are moistened, then beat on high speed 3 to 4 minutes. If beating by hand, stir until ingredients are moistened; then beat about 150 strokes per minutes for 3 to 4 minutes.
2. Butter the bottom and sides of a 3-quart glass casserole. Sprinkle sugar over the butter. Place a drinking glass open end up in the center of the dish. Remove 1 cup of batter from the bowl and save to make cupcakes. Pour remaining batter in dish around the glass.
3. Cook 10 to 12 minutes, rotating dish one-quarter turn two times, more if needed, during cooking time. A wooden pick inserted in the cake that comes out slightly moist indicates cake is done.
4. Rest cake 5 minutes until it begins to pull away from sides of dish. Remove glass from center of cake and invert cake onto serving plate. Sprinkle sifted confectioners' sugar over top, if desired.

10 to 12 servings

Note: The cake may be made in a 10-cup glass tube mold, if available.

Pineapple Upside-Down Cake

2 tablespoons butter
1 can (8 ounces) crushed pineapple
½ cup firmly packed brown sugar
6 maraschino cherries
1 package (9 ounces) yellow cake mix

1. Heat butter 30 seconds in an 8-inch round glass baking dish.
2. Drain pineapple, reserving juice.
3. Blend together butter, brown sugar, and drained pineapple; spread evenly in bottom of pan. Arrange maraschino cherries in bottom of pan.
4. Prepare cake mix as directed on package, substituting the reserved pineapple juice for water. Pour batter evenly over pineapple mixture.
5. Cook 5 to 7 minutes, rotating dish one-quarter turn halfway through cooking time. Rest 5 minutes until cake pulls away from sides of pan.
6. Invert onto serving dish.

6 to 8 servings

Note: If desired, pineapple slices may be used. Blend the melted butter and the brown sugar in baking dish and arrange slices on top. Other fruits, such as apricots or peaches, may be used, also.

Gingerbread

½ cup shortening
⅔ cup sugar
 2 eggs
⅔ cup molasses
 2 cups all-purpose flour
¾ teaspoon salt
¾ teaspoon ginger
¾ teaspoon cinnamon
¼ teaspoon baking soda
¾ cup boiling water

1. In a medium mixing bowl, cream shortening with sugar. Stir in eggs, one at a time. Gradually add molasses.
2. Combine flour, salt, ginger, cinnamon, and baking soda. Blend into creamed mixture. Add boiling water and mix until smooth.
3. Cut paper towel to line bottom of 9-inch glass baking dish. Pour batter into dish, filling no more than half full.
4. Cook 5 to 6 minutes, rotating dish one-quarter turn halfway through cooking time.
5. Rest 5 minutes before removing from pan. Serve with Lemon Sauce (page 92) or Hard Sauce (page 80).

10 to 12 servings

Note: If desired, cupcakes may be made from mixture. Use cupcaker or custard cups lined with paper baking cups. Allow 15 seconds per cupcake.

Basic Pastry Pie Shell

4 cups all-purpose flour
1 tablespoon sugar
1 teaspoon baking powder
2 teaspoons salt
1¾ cups shortening
1 egg, beaten
⅓ cup cold water
1 tablespoon cider vinegar

1. In a large mixing bowl, combine flour, sugar, baking powder, and salt.
2. Cut in shortening with a pastry blender or two knives, until particles are the size of small peas. In a 1-cup measure, combine egg, cold water, and vinegar. Stir into flour mixture until well moistened. Chill 15 minutes.
3. Divide pastry into 5 portions and form each into a ball (see Note). Flatten one ball on a lightly floured pastry cloth, and roll to about ⅛ inch thick. Ease pastry into a 9-inch glass pie plate, and flute edges.
4. Make a waxed paper starburst pattern (follow step-by-step instructions). Center waxed paper on shell and place an 8-inch glass pie plate on top.
5. Cook pastry 3 minutes. Remove 8-inch glass pie plate and waxed paper. Rotate dish one-quarter turn and cook 2½ to 3 minutes.
6. Cool on rack.

Five 9-inch pie shells

Note: If not to be used immediately, wrap balls individually in waxed paper and freeze. When needed, remove from freezer, thaw, roll, and bake as directed.

Pastry Tart Shells: Follow recipe for Basic Pastry Pie Shell. Roll one ball on floured pastry cloth, as directed. Using an inverted 10-ounce custard cup, cut out six pastry rounds. Invert six 6-ounce glass custard cups. Cover each first with a paper towel and then a pastry round. Flute each tart edge in four evenly spaced places. Place in oven in a circle and cook 4 to 5 minutes, rearranging cups one-quarter turn halfway through cooking time. Rest 3 to 4 minutes. Place upright and carefully lift out custard cup and paper towel. Cool thoroughly before filling.

6 tart shells

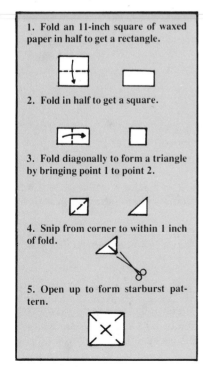

1. Fold an 11-inch square of waxed paper in half to get a rectangle.

2. Fold in half to get a square.

3. Fold diagonally to form a triangle by bringing point 1 to point 2.

4. Snip from corner to within 1 inch of fold.

5. Open up to form starburst pattern.

Walnut Torte

4 eggs
1 cup sugar
1 cup graham cracker crumbs
½ cup chopped walnuts
1 cup apricot jam
  Whipped cream

1. Beat eggs well. Combine sugar, graham cracker crumbs, and walnuts. Add to beaten eggs, mixing well. Pour into a buttered 9-inch glass cake dish with small glass, open end up, in center of dish.
2. Cook 5 to 6 minutes, rotating dish one-quarter turn halfway through cooking time.
3. Rest 5 minutes. Invert cake on plate. Spread jam over top, and serve warm or cold with whipped cream.

One 9-inch cake

Lemon Meringue Pie

1½ cups sugar
¼ teaspoon salt
1½ cups boiling water
2 tablespoons butter
6 tablespoons cornstarch
⅓ cup lemon juice
1 tablespoon grated lemon peel
3 egg yolks, slightly beaten
1 baked 9-inch pastry pie shell
3 egg whites
6 tablespoons sugar
½ teaspoon lemon juice

1. In a 4-cup glass measure, combine 1½ cups sugar, salt, water, and butter. Cook 3 to 4 minutes, stirring halfway through cooking time until sugar is dissolved.
2. Blend cornstarch with 3 tablespoons water and stir into hot sugar mixture. Cook 2 to 3 minutes, stirring after every minute.
3. Stir in ⅓ cup lemon juice and lemon peel. Gradually add egg yolks, taking care to avoid overcooking them. Cook mixture 3 to 4 minutes, stirring after every minute. Cool and pour into pie shell.
4. Using an electric mixer, beat egg whites until stiff. Continue beating while adding 6 tablespoons sugar, 1 tablespoon at a time, until rounded peaks are formed. Beat in ½ teaspoon lemon juice.
5. Spread meringue evenly over cooked filling, sealing to edges of pie shell.
6. Bake in a conventional oven at 450°F 5 to 6 minutes, or until lightly browned.

6 or 7 servings

Pumpkin Pie

1 egg, beaten
1 can (14 ounces) sweetened condensed milk
1 can (16 ounces) cooked pumpkin
½ teaspoon salt
1 teaspoon cinnamon
¼ teaspoon nutmeg

1. Combine all ingredients except pie shell. Mix until well blended.
2. Pour filling into pie shell. Cook 4 to 5 minutes until the edges begin to set. Stir the cooked edges to the center.
3. Cook 5 to 6 minutes, until the center is almost set. Rest 10 minutes. Check to see if pie is done by inserting a knife in the center. The knife should come out clean if the pie is done.

½ teaspoon allspice
¼ cup firmly packed dark brown
   sugar
1 tablespoon flour
¼ cup hot water
1 baked 9-inch pastry pie shell

4. Cool pie before serving. Top with **whipped cream** or **vanilla ice cream** and serve.

One 9-inch pie

Conventional oven: Pour filling into unbaked pastry pie shell and bake at 375°F 50 to 55 minutes.

Oatmeal Pie Crust

½ cup all-purpose flour
3 tablespoons sugar
½ teaspoon salt
⅓ cup shortening
½ cup uncooked oats
3 tablespoons cold water

1. Blend flour, sugar, and salt. Cut in shortening until particles are the size of small peas. Stir in oats.
2. Sprinkle water over mixture. Stir with a fork until dough sticks together but is not wet. Shape into a ball.
3. Flatten ball on a floured pastry cloth, and roll out to fit a 9-inch glass pie plate. Ease pastry into pie plate, and flute edge.
4. Make waxed paper starburst pattern (follow step-by-step instructions, page 83). Center waxed paper on shell and place an 8-inch glass pie plate on top.
5. Cook pastry 3 minutes. Remove waxed paper and 8-inch pie plate. Rotate dish one-quarter turn and cook 2½ to 3½ minutes. Cool.

One 9-inch pie crust

Brownie Pie

2 ounces (2 squares) unsweetened
   chocolate
2 tablespoons butter
3 eggs, beaten
½ cup sugar
¾ cup dark corn syrup
¾ cup pecan halves
1 baked 9-inch pastry pie shell

1. In a 2-cup glass measure, heat chocolate and butter 1 to 2 minutes, until melted.
2. In a large mixing bowl, combine eggs, sugar, and corn syrup; blend evenly. Slowly blend in chocolate mixture. Stir in pecan halves and pour into pie shell in glass pie plate.
3. Cook 4 to 5 minutes and rotate dish one-quarter turn.
4. Continue cooking 3 to 4 minutes until center is just beginning to set.
5. Rest pie 10 minutes. Serve slightly warm or cold with **ice cream** or **whipped cream.**

One 9-inch pie

Conventional oven: Bake at 375°F 40 to 50 minutes.

Strawberry Tarts

1 package (10 ounces) frozen
   strawberries
1 tablespoon cornstarch
   Dash cinnamon
   Dash cloves
½ teaspoon lemon juice
6 cooked pastry tart shells (page 83)
   Whipped cream (optional)

1. In a 1-quart glass casserole, cook strawberries 1 to 1½ minutes. Separate berries with a fork. Add cornstarch, cinnamon, and cloves; stir to blend evenly.
2. Cook strawberries 5 to 6 minutes, stirring after every minute, until mixture is thickened and clear. Stir in lemon juice.
3. Cool slightly and spoon into tart shells. Refrigerate until ready to serve. Top with whipped cream.

6 tarts

Fresh Strawberry Pie: Follow recipe for Strawberry Tarts. Use 4 cups fresh strawberries, cook as directed above, and pour into a **9-inch baked pastry pie shell.**

Pineapple Delight

1 cup milk
1 pound large marshmallows
1 pint whipping cream
2 cans (8 ounces each) crushed
   pineapple, drained
1½ cups graham cracker crumbs

1. In a large glass mixing bowl, heat milk 1½ to 2 minutes. When hot, stir in marshmallows; cool in refrigerator 15 minutes.
2. While mixture is cooling, beat cream until stiff peaks form.
3. Remove marshmallow mixture from refrigerator and stir in drained pineapple. Fold whipped cream into mixture.
4. Spread 1¼ cups graham cracker crumbs evenly in bottom of a 2-quart glass baking dish.
5. Pour mixture evenly over crumbs and sprinkle remaining graham cracker crumbs over top. Chill about 1 hour.

20 servings

Blueberry Tarts

1 package (16 ounces) frozen
   blueberries
½ cup sugar
2 tablespoons cornstarch
¼ teaspoon cinnamon
½ teaspoon lemon juice
6 cooked pastry tart shells (page 83)

1. In a 2-quart glass casserole, cook blueberries 1 to 1½ minutes. Separate berries with a fork. Add sugar, cornstarch, cinnamon, and lemon juice; stir to blend evenly.
2. Cook blueberries 8 to 10 minutes, stirring every 2 minutes, until mixture is thickened and clear.
3. Cool slightly and spoon into tart shells. Refrigerate until ready to serve. Top with **whipped cream.**

6 tarts

Note: If using fresh blueberries, allow 3½ to 4 cups and decrease cooking time to 6 to 8 minutes.

Quick Blueberry Pie: Follow recipe for Blueberry Tarts. Pour filling into a **9-inch baked pastry pie shell,** and allow to cool.

Congo Squares

⅓ cup butter, melted
1 cup firmly packed brown sugar
½ teaspoon vanilla extract
1 egg
1⅓ cups all-purpose flour
1¼ teaspoons baking powder
¼ teaspoon salt
¼ cup chopped walnuts
¾ cup semisweet chocolate pieces

1. In a mixing bowl, blend butter, brown sugar, and vanilla extract. Stir in egg. Combine flour, baking powder, and salt. Add to butter mixture; blend well. Stir in nuts.
2. Cover the bottom of an 8-inch square glass dish with waxed paper or paper towel. Press half the dough evenly in the bottom of the dish. Sprinkle a third of the chocolate pieces on top and press into the dough. Press remaining dough on top of chocolate pieces.
3. Cook 3½ to 4½ minutes, rotating dish one-quarter turn halfway through cooking time. Rest 5 minutes. Turn out of dish, remove waxed paper, and turn right side up.
4. Heat remaining ½ cup chocolate pieces in a glass custard cup 1 to 1½ minutes, or until soft enough to spread. Spread chocolate on top and cut into squares while warm.

16 squares

English Shortbread

½ cup butter
5 tablespoons sugar
½ teaspoon almond extract
1⅓ cups all-purpose flour
¼ teaspoon ground cloves
   Apricot jam (optional)

1. In a 1-quart glass casserole dish, heat butter 15 to 30 seconds. Stir in ¼ cup sugar and almond extract. Blend in flour with a fork, stirring until mixture is crumbly.
2. Line bottom of an 8-inch square glass baking dish with paper towel. Pour mixture into pan and press evenly over the bottom.
3. Cook 3 to 4 minutes, rotating dish one-quarter turn after every minute. In a small dish, combine 1 tablespoon sugar and cloves; sprinkle over shortbread.
4. Cut shortbread diagonally into 2×1-inch bars. Remove from dish, spread with apricot jam, and cool.

Butterscotch Bars

¼ cup butter
1 cup firmly packed brown sugar
1 egg
1 cup all-purpose flour
1 teaspoon baking powder
½ teaspoon salt
1 teaspoon vanilla extract
½ cup coarsely chopped walnuts

1. In a 1-cup glass measure, heat butter 30 seconds.
2. In a large mixing bowl, blend the butter, brown sugar, egg, flour, baking powder, salt, and vanilla extract. Fold in nuts.
3. Turn into a buttered 8-inch square glass baking dish. Cook 4 to 6 minutes, rotating dish one-quarter turn every 2 minutes.
4. Rest 5 minutes before removing from pan.

9 squares or 12 bars

Conventional oven: Bake at 375°F 25 to 30 minutes.

Almond Bark

¾ cup blanched whole almonds
1 teaspoon butter
1 package (12 ounces) semisweet chocolate pieces

1. Place almonds and butter in a 9-inch glass pie plate. Cook 3 to 4 minutes, stirring after every minute. Add more time if needed to toast almonds.
2. In a 4-cup glass measure, heat chocolate pieces 2 to 4 minutes; stir to blend. Add almonds and mix well.
3. Pour onto waxed paper and spread to desired thickness. Chill about 1 hour until firm. Break into pieces.

About 1 pound

Crispy Marshmallow Bars

¼ cup butter
4 cups miniature marshmallows
5 cups oven-toasted rice cereal

1. In a 3-quart glass casserole, heat butter and marshmallows 2½ to 3 minutes, stirring after every minute.
2. Remove from oven and add cereal, stirring until cereal is coated with warm mixture.
3. Press into buttered 11×7-inch baking dish. Cut into bars when cool.

24 large bars or 36 small bars

Chocolate Marshmallow Devils

1 package (6 ounces) semisweet chocolate pieces
15 wooden skewers
15 large marshmallows
¾ cup crushed corn chips

1. In a 2-cup glass measure, heat chocolate pieces 3 to 4 minutes, stirring well after heating.
2. Place wooden skewer in center of each marshmallow. Dip marshmallow in melted chocolate, spread with knife to coat evenly, and roll in corn chips until well covered. Chill, remove skewers, and serve.

15 coated marshmallows

Oatmeal Drop Cookies

½ cup butter
½ cup milk
2 cups sugar
¼ cup cocoa
  Pinch salt
½ cup peanut butter
1 teaspoon vanilla extract
3 cups uncooked oats

1. Heat butter and milk in a large glass mixing bowl 1 minute.
2. Stir sugar, cocoa, and salt into milk mixture. Cook 5 to 6 minutes, until it is boiling.
3. Add peanut butter and vanilla extract; stir until blended. Stir in oats.
4. Drop by spoonfuls onto waxed paper or cookie sheet. Refrigerate until firm, about 1½ to 2 hours.

4 dozen cookies

Carmelitas

32 vanilla caramels
5 tablespoons evaporated milk
¾ cup butter
¾ cup firmly packed brown sugar
½ teaspoon baking soda
¼ teaspoon salt
1 cup uncooked quick-cooking oats
1 cup all-purpose flour
1 package (6 ounces) semisweet chocolate pieces
½ cup chopped pecans

1. In a large glass mixing bowl, combine caramels and evaporated milk. Cook 2 minutes, until caramels are melted, stirring halfway through cooking time.
2. In an 11×7-inch glass baking dish, heat butter 1 minute. Combine brown sugar, baking soda, and salt with butter; mix well.
3. Stir in oats and flour. Remove ½ cup mixture; set aside. Pat remaining mixture evenly into bottom of dish.
4. Cook pressed mixture 2 to 3 minutes, rotating dish one-quarter turn halfway through cooking time.
5. Sprinkle chocolate pieces and pecans evenly over top.
6. Pour slightly cooled caramel mixture over nuts and chocolate pieces. Sprinkle reserved ½ cup oat mixture over top.
7. Cook 6 to 8 minutes, rotating dish one-quarter turn halfway through cooking time. Chill 1 to 2 hours. Cut in small pieces and store in refrigerator.

50 to 60 pieces

Note: When frozen, Carmelitas keep well for several months.

Choco-Butterscotchies

1 cup sugar
1 cup light corn syrup
1 cup peanut butter
6 cups oven-toasted rice cereal
1 package (6 ounces) semisweet chocolate pieces
1 package (6 ounces) butterscotch-flavored pieces

1. In a large glass mixing bowl, blend together sugar and corn syrup. Cook 3 to 4 minutes until mixture is boiling.
2. Stir peanut butter into hot mixture. Add cereal; stir to blend well. Press mixture into a buttered 11×7-inch glass dish.
3. In a 2-cup glass measure, heat semisweet chocolate and butterscotch-flavored pieces 2 to 2½ minutes. Stir to blend well.
4. Spread melted mixture over cereal pressed in dish. Cool about 30 minutes. Cut into 1½-inch squares, then cut each square diagonally, forming triangular pieces.

About 5 dozen pieces

Almond Drop Cookies

½ cup butter
1 cup sugar
1 egg
2 tablespoons dairy sour cream
1 teaspoon almond extract
2 cups all-purpose flour
1 teaspoon baking soda
½ teaspoon salt
  Blanched whole almonds

1. Cream butter with sugar. Stir in egg, sour cream, and almond extract.
2. Combine flour, baking soda, and salt. Stir into creamed mixture until blended.
3. Invert an 11×7-inch glass baking dish and cover with waxed paper. Drop cookie mixture by teaspoonfuls onto waxed paper, making a circle of 10 cookies one inch apart.
4. Cook 2 to 3 minutes, rotating dish one-quarter turn halfway through cooking time. Remove cookies from oven and top each with an almond. Repeat procedure with remaining batter.

40 to 50 cookies

Raisin-Stuffed Baked Apples

4 baking apples
¾ cup raisins
⅓ cup honey
1 tablespoon butter
½ teaspoon cinnamon
½ teaspoon nutmeg

1. Wash and core apples, but do not pare. Place in an 8-inch glass baking dish.
2. In a small mixing bowl, combine raisins, honey, butter, cinnamon, and nutmeg. Fill core of each apple with a fourth of the mixture. Cover pan with waxed paper.
3. Cook 6 to 8 minutes, rotating dish one-quarter turn halfway through cooking time.
4. Rest, covered, 5 minutes.

4 servings

Conventional oven: Bake at 375°F 45 minutes.

Apple Bread Pudding

3 tablespoons butter
½ cup firmly packed brown sugar
3 cups sliced cooking apples
1¼ cups applesauce
2 eggs
¼ cup milk
¼ teaspoon cinnamon
¼ teaspoon cloves
½ teaspoon salt
2 cups toasted bread cubes

1. In a 1½-quart glass casserole, heat 2 tablespoons butter 30 seconds. Sprinkle ¼ cup brown sugar over the melted butter, and arrange apple slices on top.
2. In a medium mixing bowl, combine applesauce, eggs, milk, 1 tablespoon butter, cinnamon, cloves, and salt; stir to blend. Fold in bread cubes and spread mixture over the apples.
3. Cook 5 to 7 minutes, rotating dish one-quarter turn halfway through cooking time. When a knife inserted in pudding comes out clean, the pudding should be set.
4. Rest pudding 10 minutes. Invert onto platter so apple slices are on top. Sprinkle with remaining ¼ cup brown sugar. Serve warm, topped with **vanilla ice cream** or **whipped cream.**

6 to 8 servings

Crustless Apple Pie

1½ cups sugar
1 cup all-purpose flour
2 eggs
2 teaspoons baking powder
½ teaspoon salt
½ teaspoon vanilla extract
2 cups pared and chopped cooking apples
1 cup chopped walnuts
¼ cup unsweetened pineapple juice (optional)

1. Combine all the ingredients in a large mixing bowl; blend well.
2. Pour mixture into two buttered 9-inch glass pie plates.
3. Cook each pie, one at a time, 6 to 7 minutes, rotating dish one-quarter turn halfway through cooking time.
4. Rest 10 minutes before serving.

Two 9-inch pies

Rice Pudding

2 cups evaporated milk
2 cups water
½ cup uncooked long grain white rice
3 eggs
½ cup sugar
¾ teaspoon salt
1 teaspoon vanilla extract
½ cup raisins (optional)
 Nutmeg

1. In a 1½-quart glass casserole, combine evaporated milk, water, and rice. Cook 8 to 10 minutes, or until mixture is very hot. Cover and rest 15 minutes.
2. Remove cover and cook 2 to 4 minutes, until mixture begins to bubble. Rest, covered, 15 minutes. Blend in eggs, sugar, salt, vanilla extract, and raisins. Sprinkle top with nutmeg.
3. Place hot casserole dish in an 8-inch square glass baking dish filled with 2 cups hot water. Cook 9 to 11 minutes, rotating dish one-quarter turn halfway through cooking time. Test to see if done by inserting knife in the center. The knife will come out clean when the pudding is done.
4. Serve warm or cold.

8 to 10 servings

Chocolate Pudding Cake

1 cup all-purpose flour
¾ cup sugar
2 tablespoons cocoa
2 teaspoons baking powder
½ teaspoon salt
½ cup milk
2 tablespoons shortening, melted
1 teaspoon vanilla extract
½ cup chopped walnuts
¾ cup firmly packed brown sugar
¼ cup cocoa
1¼ cups hot water
 Whipped cream

1. Sift together in a mixing bowl flour, sugar, 2 tablespoons cocoa, baking powder, and salt.
2. Stir in milk, shortening, vanilla extract, and nuts. Pour into a 9-inch square glass dish.
3. Blend together brown sugar, ¼ cup cocoa, and hot water; pour over surface of cake. Cover dish with paper towel. Cook 9 to 11 minutes, rotating one-quarter turn halfway through cooking time.
4. Rest 10 minutes before cutting. Serve warm or cold topped with whipped cream.

9 to 12 servings

Caramel Apples

5 or 6 wooden skewers or sticks
5 or 6 medium apples
1 pound wrapped vanilla caramels
1 tablespoon water

1. Push a stick in stem end of each apple. Unwrap caramels and place in a large, deep glass mixing bowl with the water.
2. Cook caramels 2 to 2½ minutes, until melted.
3. When mixture is melted, dip each apple, turning to coat with caramel.
4. Place apples on buttered waxed paper to cool. If caramel becomes too stiff to work with, heat about 1 minute, then continue dipping.

5 or 6 servings

Note: If desired, roll apples in chopped nuts immediately after coating with caramel.

Caramel Bananas

2 tablespoons milk
1 cup firmly packed brown sugar
¼ cup butter
4 large bananas

1. In a 2-cup glass measure, combine milk, brown sugar, and butter. Cook 3 to 4 minutes, stirring halfway through cooking time.
2. Slice bananas into serving dish. Pour hot mixture over bananas and serve.

4 to 6 servings

Hot Grapefruit

2 grapefruit
¼ cup firmly packed brown sugar
4 maraschino cherries

1. Prepare grapefruit for serving by cutting in half and removing seeds. Place each half in a sauce dish, cut side up. Loosen each grapefruit section with a paring knife.
2. Sprinkle 1 tablespoon brown sugar on each half. Cover each half with waxed paper and arrange in a circle.
3. Cook 2 to 3 minutes, rearranging dishes halfway through cooking time.
4. Top each half with a maraschino cherry before serving.

4 servings

Note: To cook one grapefruit half, allow 45 seconds to 1 minute cooking time.

Baked Pears

4 to 6 canned pear halves
¾ cup crushed corn flakes
2 tablespoons firmly packed brown sugar
1 tablespoon butter
Cinnamon
Cinnamon Sauce (page 93)

1. Roll pear halves in corn flake crumbs. Arrange flat side up in a 9-inch glass baking dish. Fill hollows with sugar and dot with butter.
2. Cook, covered, 3 to 4 minutes, rotating dish one-quarter turn halfway through cooking time. Sprinkle each pear half with cinnamon.
3. Serve warm with warm sauce.

4 to 6 servings

Chocolate Pudding

½ cup sugar
⅓ cup cocoa
3 tablespoons cornstarch
¼ teaspoon salt
2 cups undiluted evaporated milk
1 teaspoon vanilla extract

1. In a 4-cup glass measure, combine sugar, cocoa, cornstarch, and salt. Slowly stir in evaporated milk.
2. Cook 4 to 5 minutes, stirring after every minute, until mixture thickens. When mixture thickens, continue cooking 1 minute.
3. Add vanilla extract; stir to blend. Chill.

4 servings

Vanilla Pudding

1 egg
2 tablespoons cornstarch
¼ cup sugar
½ teaspoon salt
2 cups evaporated milk
1 tablespoon butter
1 teaspoon vanilla extract

1. In a 4-cup glass measure, beat egg. Mix in cornstarch, sugar, and salt. Stir in evaporated milk.
2. Cook 4 to 5 minutes, stirring after every minute, until mixture thickens. When mixture thickens, continue cooking 1 minute.
3. Add butter and vanilla extract; stir to blend. Chill.

4 servings

Lemon Sauce

½ cup sugar
2 tablespoons cornstarch
1 cup water
1 tablespoon butter
2 tablespoons lemon juice
1 teaspoon grated lemon peel

1. In a 2-cup glass measure, blend sugar and cornstarch. Stir in water.
2. Cook 1½ to 2 minutes, stirring halfway through cooking time, until thickened. Stir in butter, lemon juice, and lemon peel.
3. Serve warm.

About 1¼ cups

Orange Sauce: Follow recipe for Lemon Sauce, substituting **orange juice** and **orange peel** for the lemon juice and lemon peel.

Caramel Sauce

¼ cup butter
1 cup firmly packed brown sugar
⅓ cup milk or cream
2 tablespoons light corn syrup
1 teaspoon vanilla extract
　 Dash salt

1. In a 4-cup glass measure, blend butter, brown sugar, milk, and corn syrup. Cook 3 to 4 minutes, stirring every minute.
2. Add vanilla extract and salt; stir to blend. Serve warm or cold.

1½ cups

Hot Fudge Sauce or Topping

2 ounces (2 squares) unsweetened
　 chocolate
1 cup evaporated milk
1 cup sugar
½ cup butter

1. In a 4-cup glass measure, heat chocolate 2 minutes; stir well. Blend in evaporated milk and sugar. Cook 4 to 5 minutes, stirring after every minute.
2. Stir in butter. Cook 2 to 3 minutes, stirring after every minute, until mixture reaches desired consistency.
3. Serve hot over ice cream, or cool slightly and use as frosting on brownies or chocolate cake.

2 cups

Hot Buttered Rum Batter

1 pound butter
1 tablespoon brown sugar
1 tablespoon confectioners' sugar
1 teaspoon nutmeg
2 teaspoons cinnamon
1 quart vanilla ice cream, softened

1. In a large mixing bowl, soften butter 30 to 45 seconds. Blend in brown sugar, confectioners' sugar, nutmeg, and cinnamon.
2. Fold in ice cream. Pour into freezing container and freeze. Use as needed.

About 4 cups batter

Hot Buttered Rum: To make a single 1-cup serving, fill glass mug with 1 heaping teaspoon Hot Buttered Rum Batter, **1 jigger rum,** and **1 cup water.** Heat 1 to 1½ minutes. Stir to blend, sprinkle top with **nutmeg,** and serve.

Orange Glaze

2 tablespoons thinly slivered orange
   peel
¼ cup orange juice
½ cup dark corn syrup
¼ teaspoon ginger
¼ teaspoon salt

1. In a 2-cup glass measure, blend orange peel, orange juice, corn syrup, ginger, and salt. Cook 1½ to 2 minutes, stirring every 30 seconds.
2. Pour over yellow cake or use as glaze for poultry.

About ¾ cup

Conventional cooking: Combine ingredients in saucepan. Bring to boiling on top of range, and simmer 10 to 15 minutes.

Hot Cocoa

¼ cup cocoa
3 tablespoons sugar
¼ cup water
3 cups milk
   Dash salt

1. In a 1½-quart deep glass casserole, mix cocoa, sugar, and water. Cook 1 minute.
2. Slowly stir in milk, add salt, and mix well. Cook 6 to 8 minutes, stirring every 2 minutes.
3. Pour in mugs and serve hot.

3 cups

Cinnamon Sauce

1 tablespoon cornstarch
½ teaspoon cinnamon
1 cup pear juice
1 tablespoon butter

1. In a 2-cup glass measure, combine cornstarch and cinnamon. Stir in pear juice.
2. Cook 3 to 4 minutes, stirring after every minute, until mixture is thickened and clear.
3. Add butter and stir until melted.
4. Serve warm or cold over fruit, fruit salad, or cake.

About 1 cup

Irish Coffee

3 tablespoons Irish whiskey
1½ to 2 teaspoons sugar
1 tablespoon instant coffee
   Water
   Whipped cream

1. Measure whiskey into an 8-ounce coffee mug. Stir in sugar and coffee. Fill mug with water until three quarters full.
2. Cook 1½ to 2 minutes. Stir to blend. Fill with whipped cream to the brim, but do not stir in.
3. Serve immediately.

1 cup

Hot Spiced Tea

The flavor improves upon standing, so make ahead of time and heat individual servings when needed.

4 teaspoons black tea leaves
2 teaspoons whole cloves
10 cups boiling water
½ cup orange juice
1 cup lemon juice
¾ cup sugar

1. Place tea leaves and cloves in teapot or large saucepan. Pour 5 cups boiling water over tea leaves and cloves. Steep 1 hour and strain.
2. In a deep, 4-quart glass bowl, combine orange juice, lemon juice, sugar, tea, and remaining 5 cups boiling water.
3. Heat, covered, 10 to 12 minutes, stirring every 4 minutes.

12 cups

Instant Spiced Tea: Combine **2 cups water, 2 tablespoons sugar, 1 teaspoon lemon juice, ½ cup orange juice, 2 teaspoons instant tea,** and **4 whole cloves** in a 4-cup glass measure. Heat 4 to 5 minutes, stirring halfway through cooking time, and serve immediately.

2 cups

INDEX